7-18-74

Making
Leather Clothes

Making Leather Clothes

Kirsten Jørgensen

VNR VAN NOSTRAND REINHOLD COMPANY
New York   Cincinnati   Toronto   London   Melbourne

Van Nostrand Reinhold Company Regional Offices:
New York Cincinnati Chicago Millbrae Dallas

Van Nostrand Reinhold Company International Offices:
Toronto Melbourne London

This book was originally published in
Danish under the title *Skindsyning* by
Gyldendal, Copenhagen

Photographs by Andrew Stewart
Line drawings by Ole Thorsdal

Library of Congress Catalog Card
Number 73-16710
ISBN 0 442 30036 0

This book is filmset in Optima and is
printed in Great Britain by
Jolly & Barber Limited, Rugby,
and bound by the Ferndale Book Company

Published by Van Nostrand Reinhold
Company Inc., 450 West 33rd Street,
New York, N.Y. 10001, and Van Nostrand
Reinhold Company Ltd., Egginton House,
25–28 Buckingham Gate, London SW1E 6LQ

16 15 14 13 12 11 10 9 8 7 6 5 4 3 2 1

Library of Congress Cataloging in Publication Data
Jørgensen, Kirsten.
  Making leather clothes.

  Translation of Skindsyning.
  1. Leather garments.   2. Leather work.   I. Title.
TT524.J613   646.4   73-16710
ISBN 0-442-30036-0

Contents

Foreword

Man's earliest form of clothing was made of animal skins. Originally leather clothes were intended purely to protect the wearer against the weather, but before long those who made them were beginning to be more inventive and more conscious of their potential beauty. Naturally the suitability of the clothes to their purpose was the major consideration, but there is also considerable evidence of a delight in colour and a sense of the decorative. A visit to our museums is a great experience for anyone who enjoys seeing genuine craftsmanship used in the making of clothes. It goes without saying that it is even more rewarding to see this kind of handicraft in daily use, as still happens in many part of the world.

I hope this book will inspire the reader to continue the old tradition with the innovations which our present, changed conditions have brought us, and to make reasonable use of modern technical facilities. As I see it, this kind of fresh approach is sadly lacking in the traditional teaching of handicrafts and dressmaking, whether in the senior classes of primary schools or in high schools, technical colleges and evening classes.

But I have of course written this book for everyone who is interested in making clothes. I hope it will be used both as a textbook and as an inspiration to individual creativity.

Kirsten Tange Jørgensen

Leather

Despite the fact that it undergoes a number of refining processes, leather can be regarded as a natural material, and as such it has many good qualities. It is virtually indestructible. It is warm in winter and, as it is also porous, comfortable to wear in summer. It is dirt resistant, and if it does become dirty it only looks mellow. It is also pliable and soft. And, of course, it has a character and a beauty of its own. Taking all these advantages into account, leather is not expensive. The myth that leather is a luxury is due, to a certain extent, to the prices charged for ready-made leather clothes. If you make them yourself the price is comparable with that for really good fabric – high quality wool, for example, or pure silk.

When buying leather from a shop, it is essential to go to an expert who can give you advice and guidance. Leather is measured in square feet (about 30 × 30 cm.) and this includes the legs, head and so on. Take your pattern with you to the leather dealer and lay it on the skin before working out how much you are going to buy. Many skins have irregularities, small holes, thin patches, non-fast dyes and so on. Remember that leather is a natural product, so these faults don't matter; you just have to take them into account when you lay out your pattern. So it's difficult to say in advance exactly how much you will need for a particular design.

There are very few animals whose skins can't be tanned and used for a wide variety of purposes. So you will be able to find all sorts of interesting speciality skins at well-stocked leather dealers. Here, however, we shall only list the more ordinary kinds of leather which can be bought from most leather dealers. The skins of large animals are called hides, and those of smaller animals usually skins.

Different kinds of leather

Cowhide: Splendid, large hides in many lovely colours. Cowhide has weight and warmth and is suitable for cloaks, trousers etc. You can buy cowhide with both a grained and a smooth surface.

Pigskin: Golden in colour and has distinctive small bristle holes. Both sides can be used and it is phenomenally hard wearing.

Calfskin: Can be found in many varieties. In this book we have used calf suede, which is easy to sew, soft and pliable. The suede comes from the flesh side of the skin.

Suede split: Comes from calf or cowhide which is split. Split is cheap and especially suitable for children's clothes, waistcoats etc.

Lambskin: A soft supple suede with the fleece still on. However in this book it is usually used without the fleece and the word 'lambskin' merely denotes a very soft suede.

Sheepskin: Has a coarser, heavier suede than lambskin. Again it is normally used to refer to the skin with the fleece on, but unless otherwise stated it refers in this book just to the type of suede found on sheepskins. Sheepskin is very easy to work with and can be found in a large number of lovely colours. Used for dresses, waistcoats and so on.

Nappa: This leather is glossy on one side (the hair side) which is used as the right side. It is more dirt resistant than suedes. Can be made of sheep, calf, cow or goat.

Chamois or wash leather: Soft, yellow leather, usually sheepskin, from which the hair side has been split.

Glove leather: Rather thin nappa leather which is very pliable and stretchy.

Lining leather, split leather: Cheaper leather which can be used for linings, facings etc.

Leather pieces: You can buy bags of pieces or collect them yourself. There are some designs in this book which use pieces to form a kind of patchwork material.

Leather laces: Can be bought by the yard in several colours. Ready-made leather lacing wears better than home-made.

Imitation leather, artificial leather: Found in many different kinds, qualities and colours. Since these imitations are cheap you will probably find them ideal for children and young people.

Leather has no particular nap, but suede does. So when you cut out suede on a pattern make sure the nap lies the same way on every piece – it should go upwards. Leather stretches more from side to side than from head to tail, so bear this in mind when sewing gloves.

Cleaning leather

Consult a cleaners as to how to clean your garment, and always choose one that specialises in suede and leather. You can try removing any stains on suede by carefully rubbing the mark with a piece of very fine sandpaper. Some kinds of leather will also stand up to washing in soap flakes, and proprietary shampoos are available. Experiment with a remnant first.

Those designs in this book which are decorated with leather work or painted motifs may be difficult to clean. The leather dye used for the motifs will stand washing in soap flakes but not dry cleaning. So if you are using dyes on washable leather you should be able to wash the whole garment. To make sure, paint a few brush strokes of leather dye on a remnant, wash the test piece when the dye is dry and you can judge from the result how it will behave. In most cases you will be surprised to find how well it works. Wet leather articles should not be exposed to heat or sunshine. You can press leather from the wrong side with a cool iron (on the setting for nylon) but you must take great care.

If, in specific cases (the design on page 31, for example, which is for a jerkin with a painted motif) you want to be able to dry clean the garment, you may prefer to paint the motif on a circular piece of leather which can then be sewn on to the suit with running stitches, making it removable when necessary.

Sewing leather

If you are going to sew leather with a sewing machine, there are various aids you can use to make the work go more smoothly.

Sewing machine needles for leatherwork: You can buy special leather needles for all makes of sewing machine. They are triangular in section to penetrate the leather more easily.

Thread: You can sew leather with many different kinds of thread, but some kind of strengthened cotton, such as that shown in the photograph, would be ideal as it is very hard-wearing. Special waxed thread is recommended for thick

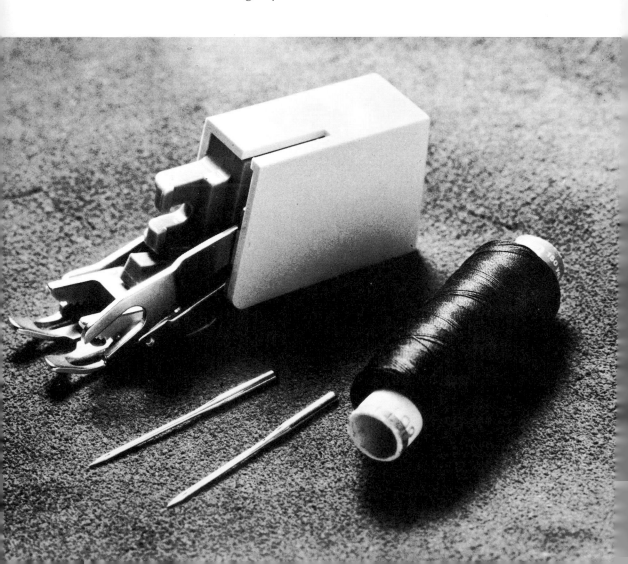

leather. For decorative stitching use buttonhole silk which will create a raised, shiny effect.

Presser foot with attachment: A very recent development on some makes of sewing machine is a special presser foot which makes it possible to sew leather easily on a domestic machine. (See illustration opposite.)

Until recently the only way to achieve satisfactory results was to use an industrial sewing machine, as some domestic machines were not capable of making regular enough stitches on leather. The presser foot should solve this problem. It can sew all kinds of seams, decorative stitching and appliqué without any difficulty. It is also very easy to operate. Eventually it should become a standard fitting on new sewing machines. All the designs in this book, however, were sewn on an ordinary machine without using a special foot.

Making up the designs

There are many different techniques which can be used when working with leather. This book aims to teach the basic or specialised ways of handling leather while taking the reader through each step in making the finished garment as shown in the designs. Through a detailed account of the process or technique being used, you should acquire both a finished garment and a knowledge of a technique which has been employed in producing something concrete. We have used the following techniques, and after each classification we have listed the garment or garments to which it is applied.

Lacing: Lime green waistcoat suit consisting of short pants and a long waistcoat.

Weaving and plaiting: Pants suit with woven skirt. Choker.

Painting on leather: Red leather jerkin with painted peasant motif.

Printing on leather: Man's and boy's waistcoats with printed motifs.

Leather combined with knitting: Dungarees with jacket and hat.

Leather combined with crochet: Chamois trouser suit.

Greenland leather embroidery I: Midi dress with traditional Greenland leather embroidery.

Greenland leather embroidery II: White nappa anorak with Greenland motif.

Greenland leather embroidery III: Red shirt and skirt. Greenland leather embroidery on the pocket.

Quilting: Pigskin skirt with quilted cable motif. Quilted chamois bikini.

Latin-American technique: Slipover with traditional Cretan pattern.

Leather mosaic: Safari suit with diamond motif in leather mosaic on the pocket.

Leather and beads: Child's dress with beadwork.

Embroidery on leather: Short evening dress with flowers embroidered on leather.

Leather with fur: Cloak trimmed with fox. Beret.

Branding leather: Boy's suit – trousers and waistcoat with branded autographs.

Appliqué I: Lambskin waistcoat with appliqué motif.

Appliqué II: Long skirt and waistcoat with appliqué flower motif.

Patchwork collage I: Long patchwork skirt.

Patchwork collage II: Jacket of leather remnants.

Leather remnants: Girl's skirt with suede patches.

Gloves: Red nappa gloves with zip.

Boots: Slipper boots.

Buttons: Examples of home-made buttons.

Braiding I: Duffle coat with braided fastening.

Braiding II: Long dress with braided belt.

After a description of the designs, including a list of materials and instructions for making them up accompanied by detailed diagrams, there follows a section on the use of the patterns. It will be helpful to read this before starting on any of the designs. For practical reasons all the patterns are together at the end of the book, and therefore each design has a reference to the page where you will find that particular pattern.

Tools

If you are working with leather as a hobby you need only acquire a fairly small number of tools. You can also use an ordinary kitchen table to work on – there is no need for a large workroom. If you only want to sew one article it is hardly worth buying any tools at all, since any leather dealer will undertake to do various jobs for a very reasonable charge. If you want to go on working in leather you will obviously find it more satisfactory to have your own tools. The most important tools for making leather clothes are the following (starting with the top left-hand corner of the photograph):

Glue: It is essential to use a really good leather glue. Ask the leather dealer which brand he recommends and follow the instructions closely. You should realise, however, that glue won't always stand up to dry-cleaning. So you will either have to sew a line of stitching to support the glue or re-stick the article after cleaning, but that won't take more than a few minutes.

Steel rule: This is handy when you're using a leather knife, as you may cut into wooden rules.

Scissors: A good pair of cutting-out scissors is essential. You

can either use fabric scissors or buy special leather scissors.

Knife: You will often find it necessary to use a knife. This should be of the Stanley knife variety – buy one with several blades so that they can be changed as they grow blunt.

Leather needle: This makes sewing leather easier. You can also buy special sewing machine needles for leather work.

Leather tracing wheel: Use this if you want to handsew a line of decorative stitching with buttonhole silk, as it will give you a uniform length of stitch.

Hole punch: A rotary punch is used for making holes. It is a revolving head with six pipes of different diameter.

Punch: When you have made a hole with the rotary punch use this implement to insert the eyelets. You can buy various pipes for the same punch.

The designs

Waistcoat suit – short pants with long waistcoat

Materials	Lime-green suede Leather lacing Press studs
Pattern	Page 116

The only decoration on this waistcoat suit, which consists of short pants and a long waistcoat, is provided by two different kinds of lacing. It is an original way of joining the pattern pieces and there are many attractive methods of lacing that may be used. The amount of sewing involved in making the garment is reduced to a minimum and can be done by hand if you don't own a sewing machine.

Waistcoat Lay the pattern on the leather. There is no need to add a seam allowance as the pieces are laid edge to edge throughout. Machine stitch the bust darts or backstitch them by hand. Use a punch to make holes along the edges of the pieces. The holes should be 1 cm. (⅜ in.) in from the edge and about the same

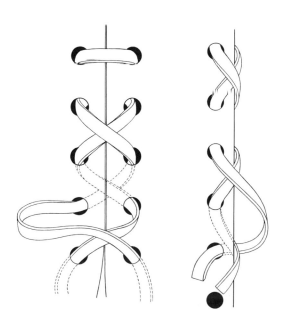

distance apart from each other. You can use scissors or a knife to cut the lacing from the suede you are using for the waistcoat, or you can buy it ready-made by the yard. Ready-made lacing is usually stronger and therefore wears better.

Start lacing up the waistcoat as shown in the diagram. It is impossible to give complete instructions as to how to finish off the lacing since this will depend on the number of holes, but try to make the overall effect as uniform as possible, passing evenly from one piece of the garment to another. End by tying a knot in the leather strips. Decorate the edges of the waistcoat with a single edge lacing, as shown in the diagram.

Short pants   Lay the pattern on the leather. Add a seam allowance for the centre front, centre back and inside leg seams. Machine stitch these seams and the darts or backstitch them by hand. Use a rotary punch to make holes along the side seams of the shorts similar to those on the waistcoat. Start lacing them together at the waist. Finish off the edges of the shorts with edge lacing. Fasten the centre front opening either with a zip, or with press studs as shown here.

Weaving Pants suit with woven skirt

Materials   Brown calf suede split
Leather lacing
2 zips, each 20 cm. (8 in.) long
3 hook fastenings

Pattern   Page 117

Draw up the pattern on squared paper. Lay it on the leather, add the seam allowance and cut out the various pieces.

Overblouse   Tack the darts and seams. Tack in the sleeves and try on the overblouse. Assuming it fits without further cutting, machine stitch together. Neaten the neck opening with a facing. Lay this right side down on the right side of the blouse, stitch and turn to the wrong side. Lace the bottom edge of the blouse with a row of single edge lacing. Use a punch to make holes ½ cm. (³/₁₆ in.) apart and the same distance in from the edge of the leather. You can either make the lacing from the leather used for the overblouse or buy it ready-made from a leather dealer. Lace along the edge as shown in the diagram below. You can decorate the bottom edges of the sleeves with 'figures of eight'. Using the diagram on the next page as a pattern, draw these on the leather, cut them out and put them through slits cut in the sleeves. It will be obvious from the diagram how to do this.

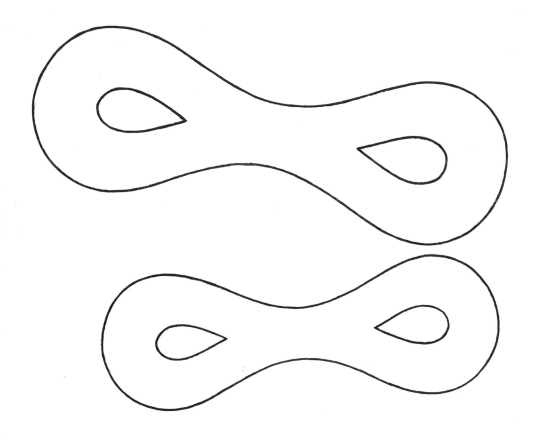

Pants   Tack all darts and seams. Attach the waistband to the pants. Now try them on. This fitting is very important. The pants should be shaped closely to the body. Any extra width should be taken in at the darts, the side seams and the centre back seam. When the pants fit really well machine stitch them together. Sew on the waistband with two lines of stitching from the outside. Set a zip in the centre front. Fasten the waistband with a hook and eye. Finish the top edge of the pants with the same kind of lacing used for the overblouse.

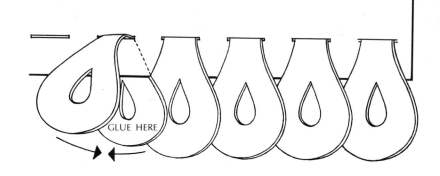

GLUE HERE

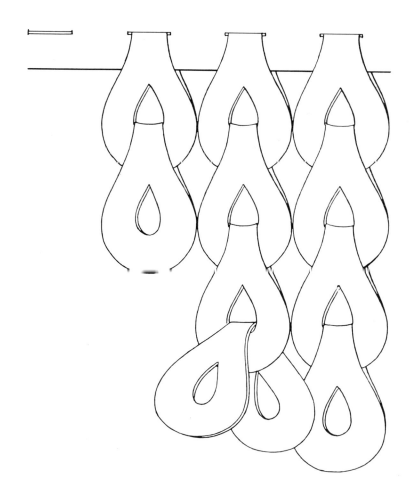

Skirt   Tack together the two halves of the skirt yoke and try on. Then stitch the side seams. Strengthen the bottom edge of the yoke with a piece of leather 3 cm. (1⅛ in.) wide, cut to shape and glued to the wrong side of the yoke. Edge the waist with the same kind of lacing used for the overblouse and pants. Draw a larger number of 'figures of eight' on the leather, using the larger of the two diagrams as a guide. Note that for this you can use up all the bits of leather you are bound to have left over from cutting out the main pattern pieces. Now use a leather knife to make slits through which to pass the 'figures of eight', and proceed to weave the skirt (see diagram on the preceding page). When the skirt has reached the required length stick down the last row of 'figures of eight' with a blob of glue. You can of course also make a 'mini' skirt, but in that case you should cut the yoke to about 10 cm. (4 in.) deep and shorten each length of weaving. When you have finished the weaving fasten the skirt at the front with three flat hook fastenings.

Plaited choker

Materials Blue-green sheepskin without the fleece
1 button
Pendant (a stone, say, or a locket)

We have included this kind of plaiting because it can be used for so many things: belts, for example, bracelets, handles and so on. It has therefore become something of a classic technique.

Choker Cut a strip of leather about 3 × 37 cm. (1⅛ × 15 in.). The longer of these two measurements will naturally depend on the neck size. If you want the plaiting wider alter the first measurement. Using scissors or a knife, cut this piece of leather in the following way: leaving 3 cm. (1⅛ in.) uncut at each end of the leather strip, mark out with a biro on the wrong side of the leather three equal-sized strips, each 1 cm. (⅜ in.) wide. Cut along these lines. Now you can start the actual plaiting.

The procedure for plaiting is shown on page 71, but the difference here is that the ends are not loose as in the diagram but joined together in the uncut 3 cm. (1⅛ in.) wide pieces at each end of the strip. So while plaiting at one end, you will have to 'unravel' the plaiting at the other. It is impossible to illustrate this in a diagram as it would be too complicated, but it is not at all difficult in practice. You just have to check continually that the bottom end of the leather is lying smooth before carrying on with the plaiting at the top. When you have plaited the leather strip right through, sew a button on to one end and make a buttonhole in the other so that you can fasten the choker round the neck. You can use whatever you have available as a pendant. Here we have attached a little amber heart.

Red leather jerkin with painted peasant motif

Materials	Red suede split Leather dyes – white, yellow, blue and green 4 buckles Leather lacing
Pattern	Page 118

Draw the pattern on to tissue paper, lay it on the suede and cut out the jerkin. The motif used here was inspired by Norwegian peasant designs. It is better to paint it on before sewing the jerkin together. But leather dyes in white, yellow, blue and green from your leather dealer. Now paint the motif from the diagram with a brush; start by practising on remnants. You may find that you have to draw the brush backwards and forwards before the dye completely covers the leather. The motif will look more effective if the paint is not applied absolutely evenly. Leather dyes are also available in felt-tipped tubes. They are easier to use, but the result is not as fine.

Jerkin Tack the darts and seams and try on. Stitch the half belt together. Stitch the darts and seams, sewing the sides of the half belt into the side seams at waist level. Fold over the front edges to the wrong side and glue down. If the jerkin is too tight over the hips, all you need do is leave the bottom of the side seams open for about 10 cm. (4 in.) to make two slits. Finish the neck opening, arm openings and the bottom edge of the jerkin with leather lacing. Cut the lacing from the same leather as the jerkin, punch holes about ½ cm. (³/₁₆ in.) in from the edge and about the same distance apart, and use the method of lacing shown on page 23. Fasten the jerkin at the centre front with purchased buckles.

Man's waistcoat with printed motif

Materials   Fudge-coloured suede split
Leather dye – dark brown
Leather lacing
Lino printing block 5 × 5 cm. (2 × 2 in.)
Lino-cutting tool
Zip, 40 cm. (16 in.) long

Pattern   Page 119. Chest measurement about 100 cm. (40 in.).

Waistcoat   Lay the pattern pieces on the leather. There is no need for an extra seam allowance. Cut out along the edges of the pattern. Punch holes about 1 cm. (⅜ in.) apart and ¾ cm. (¼ in.) in from the edge of the leather. Lace the waistcoat together along the centre back with leather lacing cut from the suede split, using the method of lacing shown here.

Then sew facings to the neck opening, the arm openings and the bottom edge of the waistcoat. Machine stitch them at the width of the pressure foot from the edge. You can now join the side seams with the same kind of lacing as for the centre back.

Printing   Now decorate the shoulder flaps with leather printing. Most hobby shops stock lino blocks measuring 5 × 5 cm. (2 × 2 in.), ready for use. After drawing the pattern on to this block, using carbon paper if you wish, cut the pattern out with special lino cutting tools so that it is raised and the outline clear. Then cut all the surplus lino away.

The actual printing is done in the following way: put a piece of foam rubber into an old dish and wet the foam rubber thoroughly with the leather dye. You can buy the dye in any shoe shop or leather merchant's. Then take the printing block and press it lightly several times on the pad. The pattern should be saturated with dye. Any dye which has run on to the edges of the block can be wiped off with a rag. Try a few practice printings. When you have mastered the technique, print on the actual shoulder flap. Decorate the edges of this with lacing. Make holes about 1 cm. (⅜ in.) apart and ½ cm. ($^3/_{16}$in.) in from the edge of the flap and proceed according to the diagram.

Glue the shoulder flap on to the waistcoat. You can now join the shoulder seams with the same form of lacing as for the centre back. Finish the lacing off with a knot or bow. Hand or machine sew a zip into the centre front. Cover the tag of the zip with a tassel of leather strips.

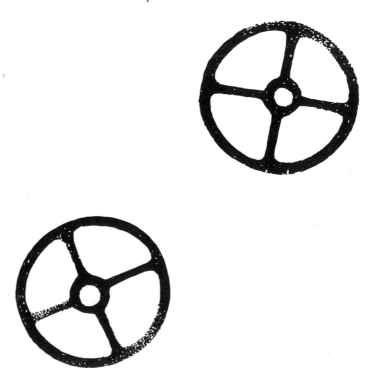

Laced edging on shoulder flap

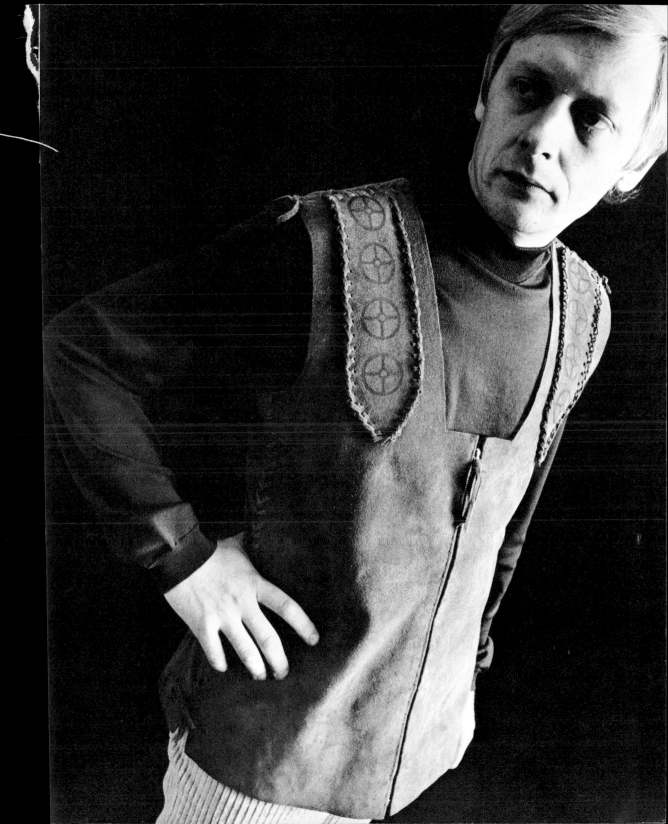

Boy's waistcoat with printed motif

Materials	Lime-green suede
	Leather dye – dark green
	Leather lacing
	2 lino blocks
	Lino-cutting tools

Pattern Page 120. Size about 7 years.

Waistcoat Cut out from the pattern. No seam allowance need be made. Fringe the yoke with scissors or a knife, then machine stitch it on to the waistcoat. Cut the fringed edging out, clip the fringes with a knife or with scissors and stitch the fringe on to the waistcoat.

Technique for printing on leather We have already described this on page 34 so there is no need to repeat it here. The motif used on the man's waistcoat is the same as that used on the front of the boy's waistcoat. The back is decorated with a gazelle lying down, a mid-15th century motif found in the German National Museum in Nuremberg. We have used green leather dye on this model.

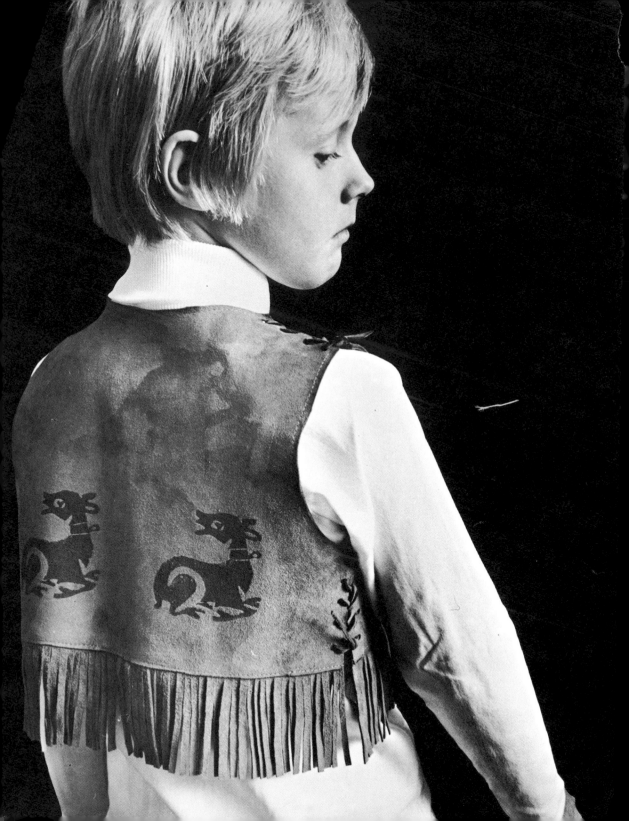

If it looks as if the armholes on the waistcoat will need to be strengthened, you can cut out a facing and machine stitch it in place. Finish the waistcoat by punching holes along the shoulder and side seams, about 1 cm. (⅜ in.) apart and ¾ cm. (¼ in.) in from the edge of the leather. Lace these seams together with leather lacing cut from the same suede you have used for the waistcoat. It should be about ½ cm. (³⁄₁₆ in.) thick. The method of lacing used is the same as that on page 33.

Dungarees with jacket and hat

Materials Dark red cowhide
2 buckles
12 50 gm. (22 oz.) balls of black 4-ply crepe wool
Knitting needles, size 9 and 11
2 zips, 20 cm. and 55 cm. long (8in. and 22 in.)

Pattern Pages 121–122

Trousers Draw up the pattern and lay it on the hide. Now tack all darts and seams and try the trousers on. If they fit properly machine stitch all darts and seams. Before going on to attach the facing you must decide whether you want the bib and braces to be removable. If this is the case, put press studs in the back of the waistband as shown on the pattern. Attach the waistband as follows: lay the waistband on the trousers, right sides together, stitch and turn the band to the wrong side. Hem stitch it down. Cut the bib double. You can use slightly thinner leather for this if you wish. Place the bib and the bib lining right sides together. Now cut two strips of leather 4 cm. (1½ in.) wide and 10 cm. (4 in.) long. Thread these round the buckles. Take the strips used to attach the buckles and lay them between the back and front of the bib with the buckles inside. This way they will be caught in when you stitch along the two side seams and the top edge of the bib. Now turn the bib right side out and the buckles will be in the right position. Finish the bib by setting the other half of the press studs in the bottom so that they will fit into the half you have put in the waistband. Cut out the braces from the pattern – they should be double thickness. As they would be too awkward to turn inside out, glue the two pieces together. Attach them with press studs to the centre back of the waistband.

Jacket The fronts of the jacket are cowhide. Cut them out from the pattern and keep to one side until you've finished the rest of the jacket. Knit the back and sleeves in raised rib as follows:
1st row: knit 1, wool forward, slip 1 loosely purlwise, repeat to the last 2 stitches, knit 2.
2nd row: knit 1, * wool forward, slip 1 loosely purlwise, knit 1 taking the next stitch and the loop together, repeat from * to last stitch, knit 1. The second row creates the raised rib, so repeat this.

Back	Using no. 11 needles, cast on 100 stitches and work 7 cm. (2¾ in.) twisted rib as follows: knit 1 through the back of the loop, plain 1, repeat to end. Change to no. 9 needles and work in raised rib till the back measures 35 cm. (14 in.) from the cast on edge. Cast off 3 stitches at the beginning of the next 2 rows. On the following 10 rows decrease 1 stitch at both ends of every other row. Then decrease 1 stitch at both ends of every row 30 times. There should now be 24 stitches left on the needle. Cast off.
Sleeves	Using no. 11 needles, cast on 50 stitches. Work 7 cm. (2¾ in.) twisted rib as for the back. Change to no. 9 needles and proceed in raised rib. Cast on 1 stitch at both ends of every eighth row until there are 88 stitches on the needle. Continue straight until the work measures 52 cm. (21 in.) from the cast on edge. Now decrease as described for the back. Cast off the remaining 12 stitches.
Fronts	Using no. 11 needles, cast on 50 stitches and knit 7 cm. (2¾ in.) twisted rib. Cast off. Then knit another piece the same for the other front. Now take the leather fronts and stitch the bust darts.
Making up the jacket	Press the knitted work lightly on the wrong side. Backstitch the jacket together with the black knitting wool. Start by sewing the rib borders for the leather fronts to the lower edge of the jacket. Continue by sewing up the side seams between back and fronts. Lay the back about 1 cm. (⅜ in.) over the edge of the leather front and stitch firmly. Sew the sleeve seams and set them into the armholes. Lay the sleeves over the edge of the leather at the front and stitch firmly. Set the sleeves into the back arm opening.
Collar	Using no. 11 needles, cast on 111 stitches and work in twisted rib for 7 rows. Now decrease 1 stitch at both ends of every other row 12 times. Work another 2 rows without shaping. Cast off 5 stitches at the beginning of the next three rows and 10 stitches at the beginning of the next two rows. Cast off the remaining stitches.
Finishing	Press the collar and sew it into the jacket. The best way to do this is by sewing it in from the wrong side with buttonhole stitch. Stitch right through the leather on the fronts. Set the longer zip in the front of the jacket with invisible stitches.
Hat	Using no. 11 needles, cast on 100 stitches. Work 7 cm. (2¾ in.) twisted rib. Now change to raised rib and no. 9 needles. Work 17 cm. (7 in.). Change back to no. 11 needles and knit 7 cm. (2¾ in.) twisted rib. Thread the wool through the stitches and gather up the top of the hat. Add a pompom if you wish.

Chamois trouser suit

Materials
Good quality, firm chamois
Linen yarn – red, dark green and light green
Crochet hook no. 3½ (1 mm.)
5 gold hooks
Zip, 20 cm. (8 in.) long

Pattern
Page 123

When you have drawn up the whole pattern lay it on the leather. Add the seam allowance and cut out the suit.

Blouse
Tack the darts and seams and try on the top. Machine stitch together. Turn the centre front facing to the wrong side. Punch holes about ½ cm. (³/₁₆ in.) apart and the same distance in from the edge of the leather, in the neck opening, the arm holes and round the bottom edge of the blouse. Now crochet the edging in three colours using the no. 3½ crochet hook. For the crochet use linen yarn in light green, red and dark green.

Start with a row of double crochet over the edge of the leather as follows: push the hook through the hole in the leather, yarn round hook, pull stitch through the hole. Yarn round hook and pull the thread through the stitch you have just made and the one before, which is also on the hook. Use the light green colour for the first row. Then crochet a row of red double crochet in the following way: hook through the last stitch of the row before, yarn round hook and pull through the stitch, yarn round hook again and pull through both stitches. To finish the border, crochet a row of dark green picots. Make three chains, then double crochet into the first chain. Attach the picot by a double crochet stitch through the last stitch of the row before. Work this strip of crochet at the neck opening and arm openings. At the bottom edge of the blouse work as follows: two rows in light green, two rows in red and two rows dark green double crochet. Finish the bottom edge with a row of dark green picots. Fasten the blouse with four hooks.

Trousers
Tack the darts and seams and try on the trousers. Ideally, they should fit like a second skin. Then machine stitch all darts and seams. Crochet the waistband as follows: make a row of chain

stitches in dark green yarn long enough to fit about 5 cm. (2 in.) below your own waist measurement. If the belt comes out too long you can always shorten it later by making a line of zigzag stitches with the sewing machine across the belt at the required length, and cutting off the unwanted piece. Now crochet one row of dark green double crochet into the row of chain stitches, then one row red, one row light green, one row red and one row dark green. Edge the waistband with a row of dark green picots on both sides. Place this so that the top row of picots lies over the edge of the trousers. Using sewing silk the colour of the chamois, sew on the belt with a line of invisible running stitches along the edge of the waistband. Make one tiny stitch in each picot of the bottom row. Turn the band to the wrong side of the trousers at the centre front. Then set in a zip by hand and fasten the belt with a hook.

Crochet the flare for the trousers as follows: punch a row of holes about ½ cm. ($^3/_{16}$ in.) apart and ¾ cm. (¼ in.) in from the edge of the leather. Since the crochet work here is rather heavy, turn up the bottom edge of the trousers 2 or 3 cm. (about 1 in.) on the wrong side so that you can punch the holes through two thicknesses. Begin with light green yarn as for the blouse. Then crochet round the trouser leg, four rows light green double crochet, four rows red double crochet and four rows dark green double crochet. Repeat this sequence five times. As you work, increase by crocheting twice into the same stitch. It is virtually impossible to specify exactly when and how often to increase as this will depend on the number of stitches and the firmness of the crochet. If you make a pattern from the diagram you can match the crochet against it as you work. Lay the trousers together seam to seam, place the pattern underneath and make sure the trousers flare out in a straight line. Finish with a row of dark green picots. Lastly, press in light creases at the centre front and back of the crochet flare.

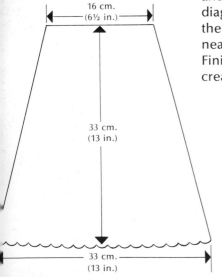

16 cm.
(6½ in.)

33 cm.
(13 in.)

33 cm.
(13 in.)

Leather bag of de-haired sealskin, West Greenland, c. 1840 (National Museum of Denmark) – opposite

Midi dress with Greenland leather embroidery

Materials   1 blue cowhide
Leather lacing – red and white
Zip, 55 cm. (22 in.) long

Pattern   Page 124

The trimmings on this dress are based on a traditional em-

broidery technique from Greenland, which you can see illustrated here. It is easy to do and can be used on many different articles.

Dress Copy the pattern on to paper – you can make a shorter version if preferred. Lay your paper pattern on the leather and add the seam allowance. Then cut out the dress. The leather used for this design is comparatively heavy, but it makes a marvellously warm dress for winter wear. For summer you would need to use a lighter quality. Tack the dress together and try it on. If it fits, machine stitch all darts and seams.

Greenland embroidery We have used the threaded pattern on the belt and the collar. Buy ready-made leather lacing in white and red. Using a steel rule, make small slits in the leather, as shown in the diagram. You must work very carefully, but as long as your leather knife is sharp enough the actual cutting is easy. When you have made all the slits, draw the lacing through using a bodkin or a darning needle.

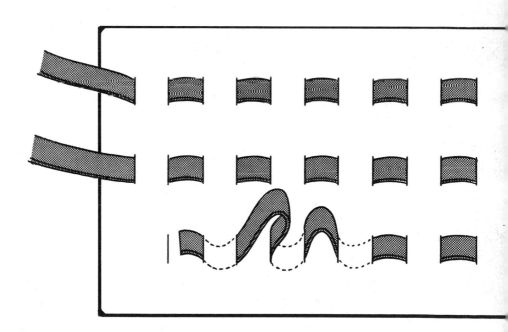

Making up the dress When you have finished embroidering the collar sew it on to the dress. Fold the collar right sides together and stitch the ends. Turn and lay it down, right side on the right side of the dress neck opening. Stitch firmly in place. Fasten the inside of the collar to the wrong side of the neck opening with small hemstitches or with glue. Set the zip in the centre back of the dress. Glue up the bottom edge.

Belt Use the same technique as for the collar, but let the ends of the lacing hang loose so that you can fasten the belt by tying them together. Neaten the inside of the belt by folding the seam allowance back to the wrong side and glueing a layer of leather over it.

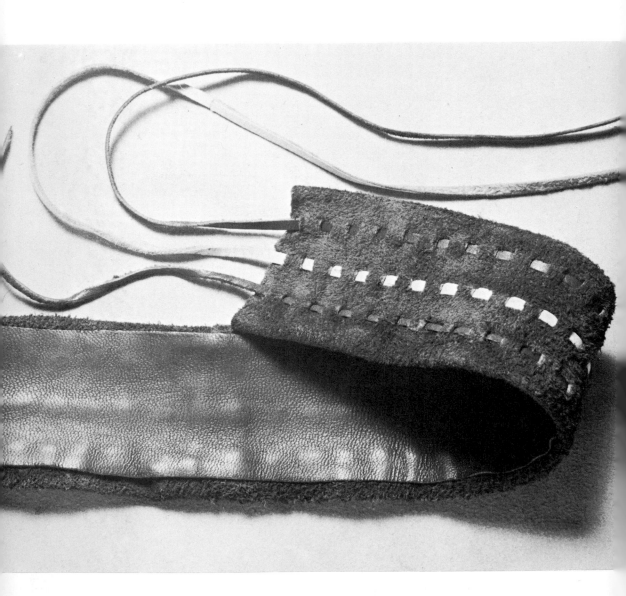

White anorak with Greenland motif

Materials	White Persian nappa leather Nappa pieces – green, blue, red and black White lacing Eyelets
Pattern	Page 125
Anorak	Draw up the pattern and lay it on the leather. Add the seam allowance and cut out the anorak. Do not close the sleeve seams but place the top of the sleeves over the arm opening and join them, right sides together. Sew a line of decorative

stitching the width of the presser foot from the first line of stitching. Before completely making up the anorak attach the hood, which should be lined, and preferably with the same leather as used for the anorak. However if you want to save money use white canvas or linen. Stitch the two centre seams on the hood, over the top and at the front. Place the hood and the lining right sides together and stitch right round the opening for the face. Turn the hood. If you want to be able to open the hood right out at the front, insert the eyelets at the centre front. Stitch the hood to the anorak. Lay the wrong side of the hood on the right side of the anorak and attach it with two rows of stitching. Leave the width of the presser foot between the two rows of stitching. Now you can sew up the remaining seams on the anorak. Start by tacking the side and sleeve seams. Make sure that the stitching on the arm opening matches on both the front and the back of the anorak. Stitch the side and sleeve seams. Glue up the sleeve hems and the bottom of the anorak.

Greenland leather embroidery

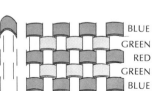

BLUE
GREEN
RED
GREEN
BLUE

Traditionally, the strips of leather used for the embroidery are only 1½ mm. ($\frac{1}{16}$ in.) thick. To simplify the task, we have increased them to ½ cm. ($\frac{3}{16}$ in.). Cut the strips with a knife or scissors. Then draw up the pattern of the pocket flap on to greaseproof paper and attach it to the back of the pocket flap with Sellotape. Use a leather knife to make small slits in the leather, as shown in the diagram, about 1 mm. ($\frac{1}{25}$ in.) apart to ensure that the various strips of leather remain separate. When you have finished cutting out the pattern, pull the strips of leather through with a bodkin or darning needle. Stick down the ends on the wrong side with a little glue. When you have finished the embroidery, back the pocket flap with black glove leather, letting it overlap the edge of the pocket flap by about 1 cm. (⅜ in.). Decorate this edge with small notches of the kind found on Greenland kamiks, or sealskin boots (see illustration). Finally, attach the pocket flap to the anorak.

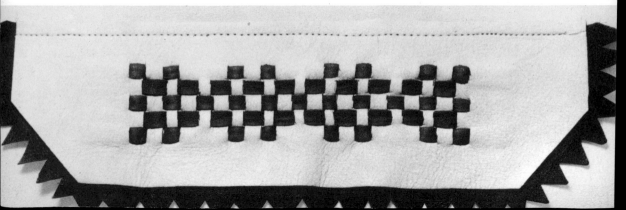

Red shirt and skirt with Greenland leather embroidery

Materials   Red nappa glove leather
Strips of nappa glove leather – white, black, blue, red, yellow and green
Zips, 20 cm. (8 in.), 45 cm. (22 in.) and 2 10 cm. (4 in.) long

Pattern   Page 126

The only trimming on this suit is the Greenland leather embroidery which is taken from a traditional Greenland costume. The original is illustrated in the photograph below, which shows a detail of the embroidery on the front of a pair of women's trousers. It may look difficult, but it is fascinating to do.

When buying leather for this kind of embroidery you must make sure that it isn't too soft. This is to prevent the embroidery looking untidy, because the edges of soft leather strips would turn up. In Greenland they use hand-dressed leather as it is very stiff, but you can use nappa as long as it isn't too soft.

Traditional leather embroidery from Greenland national costume

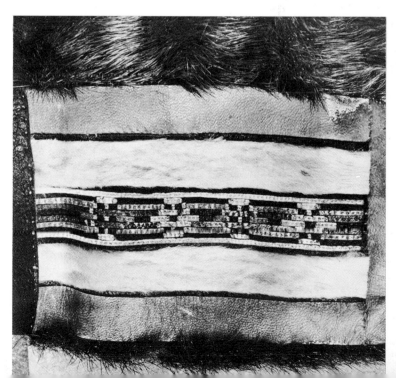

Close-up of leather embroidery on pocket

Shirt   Draw up the pattern, add the seam allowance and cut out the shirt. Tack the darts and seams and try on the shirt. If it fits, machine stitch the darts and the side and sleeve seams. On some machines it may be difficult to stitch thin glove leather of this kind. However, if you place some tissue paper under the seam as you sew, the machine will pick up the leather more easily. Remove the tissue paper after stitching. Turn the centre front edge to the wrong side and attach the collar. You may have difficulty getting fine, even points on the collar, but if you decide to use some pointed object to help push the points through when you turn the collar, you should be especially careful not to poke it through the leather. Stitch the under collar to the jacket. Using invisible hemming stitches sew the top collar to the inside of the shirt along the line of machine stitching. Glue up the sleeve hems and set two zips in the slits. Fasten the shirt with a zip at the centre front.

Skirt Draw up the skirt pattern, add the seam allowance and cut out. Tack the darts and side seams. Try the skirt on and then stitch. Attach the waistband and set a zip in the side seam. Glue up the bottom edge.

Greenland leather embroidery Cut out a piece of black nappa measuring 2½ × 12 cm. (1 × 5 in.). It is advisable to add a seam allowance to both of these measurements as it is impossible to say exactly what size the finished embroidery will be. Then use a leather knife and a steel rule to cut out some strips in white, blue, yellow, green and red nappa. Each strip should be 2 mm. ($^1/_{10}$ in.) wide. Now, following the diagram, stitch the small leather strips in place, handsewing with almost invisible stitches and using thread which exactly matches the colour of the leather. The stitches should be very close together.

Take each strip of leather separately and start stitching it in place at one end. Then cut the strip off with a leather knife when you have sewn enough according to the diagram. This is easier than having tiny little pieces of leather to cope with. When you have finished the embroidery cut out the black nappa backing to form an edge and place it on the pocket, turning the ends to the wrong side. The pocket is cut double to take the embroidery. Stitch it on to the shirt by hand with little invisible stitches.

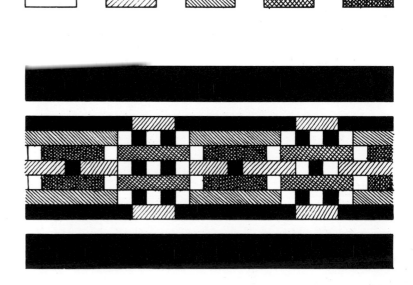

WHITE   YELLOW   RED   GREEN   BLUE

Pigskin skirt with quilted cable motif

Quilting

Materials
2 pieces golden pigskin
Buckle
Eyelets
Gauze
Quilting thread
Zip, 20 cm. (8 in.) long

Pattern
Page 127

Draw up the skirt pattern and lay it on the leather. Add the seam allowance and cut out the skirt.

Quilting
Make two copies of the cable motif on tissue paper. For the quilting you will need to buy gauze or other equally thin material. Special quilting thread may be difficult to obtain, and if so you can use thick wool instead. Lay the gauze over the centre front of the skirt on the wrong side and cover it with the tissue paper on which you have drawn the motif. Stick all these layers together with Sellotape. Then, still from the wrong side, machine stitch along the outline of the motif, using thread a little lighter in colour than the pigskin. Remember to leave fairly long threads hanging whenever you have to stop the stitching and start again, so that you can pull them through to the wrong side and fasten them off afterwards. When you have done both fronts of the skirt, pull off the tissue paper. Then use a darning needle to outline the cable motifs with two or three thick threads. This will produce a relief effect on the right side.

Skirt
Tack the darts and seams and try the skirt on. After making any adjustments, machine stitch the skirt together. Cut out the belted waistband and buy a buckle. Machine stitch a 20 cm. (8 in.) zip in the centre front seam to fasten the skirt. Allow about 4 cm. (1½ in.) for attaching the buckle to the belt. Fold this piece round the buckle and fasten it with metal rivets. Attach the belted waistband to the skirt by laying the right sides of the waistband and skirt together, machine stitching along the length of the skirt waist, turning the waistband to the wrong side and sewing it down. Insert the eyelets in the loose

piece of the waistband to make a little belt which can be buckled. Finally, turn up the hem of the skirt and glue in place.

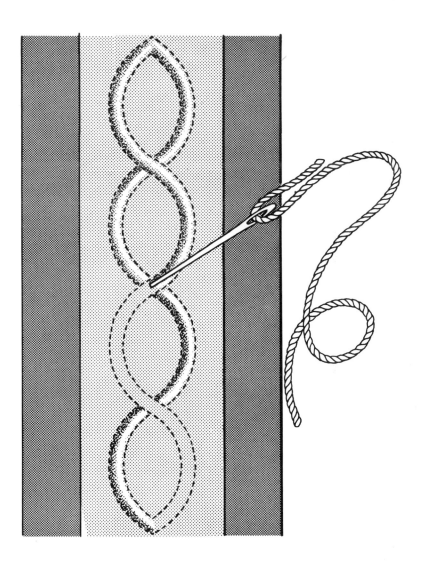

Quilting Quilted chamois bikini

Materials Chamois leather
White quilted nylon lining
5 button trims
White bias binding
Elastic fastening with clasp for the bra
Wire cup shapes, if required

Pattern Page 128

Add the seam allowance to the pattern and cut out.

Quilting The disadvantage of chamois leather is its tendency to stretch during use, especially if it gets wet. So we have used the quilting for two purposes – it is decorative and it will also keep the leather in shape. Buy quilted nylon lining in a material shop. Lay it under the various pieces of the bikini, wrong sides together, and machine stitch along the quilting lines already in the lining using thread the same colour as the chamois. It is quite an easy job, but take care that the leather isn't being stretched on the right side. You can prevent this by changing

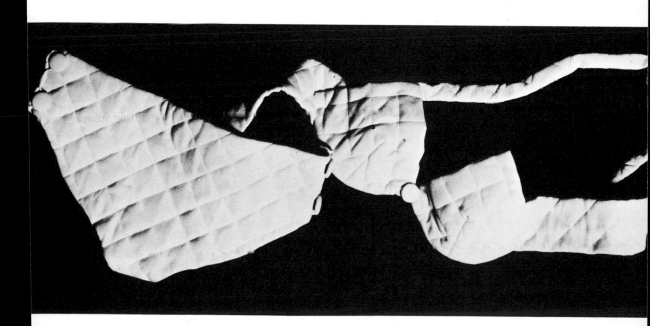

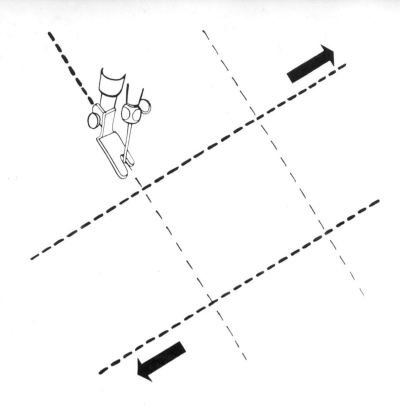

the direction of the sewing for each line of quilting (see the diagram above). Quilt all the pattern pieces in the same way.

Pants   Trim the lining along each edge. Lay white bias binding with the right side on the right side of the pants and stitch it along the edge of each piece. Turn the seam allowance and the binding to the wrong side and stitch the binding down with invisible hemming. Fasten the pants with matching covered chamois buttons which you can make yourself (see the instructions on page 111). Handsew loops on to the front of the pants.

Bra   Trim the nylon lining. Tack the dart in the middle of the cup and stitch. Neaten the seams with bias binding as for the pants. When all the pieces are finished try the bikini on. How you finish the bra will depend on your own taste and requirements. If you want to support the bust you can buy two wire shapes and sew them into the bottom edge of the cups. When you have fitted the bra sew the individual pieces together by hand and attach a bra fastening, which you can buy ready-made, at the centre back. Sew on a button for decoration at the centre front.

Slipover with Cretan pattern

Latin-American technique

Materials   Light golden sheepskin without the fleece
Suede remnants – red, blue and greyish-green
Zip, 45 cm. (18 in.) long, opening at both ends

Pattern   Page 128

Draw up the pattern and lay it on the leather. Add a seam allowance for the side seams and cut out the slipover.

Latin-American technique   The motif in this design is a very old one originating in Crete, and well suited to this technique. The illustration below shows a child's dress from Panama which was made by simply placing

Girl's dress from the San Blas Islands, Panama (National Museum of Denmark)

LIGHT GOLD  RED  GREYISH-GREEN  BLUE

64

four or five layers of material in different colours under each other and then cutting down into the material, thereby achieving a kind of appliqué effect in reverse. For this model we have used leather in blue, greyish-green and red as well as the light golden colour of the actual slipover.

Cut out the different steps in the pattern from the diagram, glue the whole lot together and place it in a circle cut out of the slipover. Glue won't stand up to wear in this case, so you will have to fasten the motif round the edge with almost invisible stitches, using thread exactly the same colour. Place the light gold piece as a kind of background to the pattern in the centre of the motif to create the golden 'flower'. Cheat with the blue blob in the centre by attaching it on top of the gold piece. Make sure that you don't buy too thick a suede for this technique as it will be hard to sew through so many layers.

Slipover   Tack the darts and side seams and try on. If it fits, machine stitch it together. Edge the neck opening, the bottom hem and the arm openings with a strip of the same leather as the slipover. Cut this 3 cm. (1⅛ in.) wide, and sew it on by hand with small stitches which should be almost invisible from the right side. Fold the strip over the edge and stitch through all three layers. If you use a good thimble the work should be fairly easy. Set a zip in the centre back. You should use the kind of zip which will open at the bottom.

Safari suit with diamond motif in leather mosaic

Leather mosaic

Materials 2 pieces of putty-coloured calf suede
Suede pieces – red, golden, green and blue
Belt buckle
10 buttons
Zip, 20 cm. (8 in.) long

Pattern Pages 129–130

You should probably only tackle this design if you have some experience of dressmaking, but if not you can always consult a detailed guide to sewing techniques. There are many good books on the subject, and you may find one in your local library. Obviously you can use the leather mosaic technique for much more unusual designs. Draw up all the pattern pieces and lay them on the leather. Add the seam allowance and cut out.

Skirt Tack the skirt together and try it on. After making any adjustments necessary, machine stitch. Set in the zip and finish by attaching the waistband.

Leather mosaic As the breast pockets are included in one of the first seams to be stitched on the suit, you should start with the leather

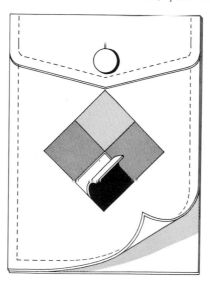

mosaic. The pockets are cut double; using a sharp leather knife cut out a square 5 × 5 cm. (2 × 2 in.) from one layer of each pocket. The two layers with the squares cut out of them become the outer layer of each breast pocket.

Now cut for each pocket four small squares measuring 2½ × 2½ cm. (1 × 1 in.) in different colours. We have chosen red, blue, green and yellow, but the choice of colours is of course up to you. Place these small squares in the larger square cut out of the pocket, and glue to the front of the pocket. Be careful when you start the glueing that the small squares fit exactly together without any gaps between them.

Jacket You can now stitch the pockets to the jacket. Cut the pocket flaps double as well, and join the two layers with a line of machine stitching. Then tack the pocket flaps firmly into the seam line of the yoke and front. Machine stitch these seams. Sew up the centre back seam and stitch the back yoke and back together. Make the pleat in the centre back as you are stitching the centre back seam. It is advisable to tack the jacket together now and try it on. This will ensure that it fits really well. After this fitting you can machine stitch the main body of the jacket together.

As you can see from the photograph the lapel has been cut with the smooth side of the leather as the right side. Start by stitching the front facing to the jacket, right sides together. Turn the facing to the wrong side. Cut the collar double, stitch the two pieces together and turn. Now attach the collar. Stitch on the under collar from one end to the other. Handsew the top collar to the lapel with invisible stitches. Attach the centre of the collar to the neck of the jacket. Tack in the sleeves and try the jacket on again. Then stitch in the sleeves and finish them with a single turn up of the smooth side of the leather to make a cuff. Cut the big pockets singly. Glue the pleat down on the wrong side and machine stitch the pockets to the jacket. The pockets flaps are double. Stitch them together and on to the jacket. Glue up the bottom hem of the jacket. Cut the belt to the desired length. Glue it to a stiff backing. On this model we have used a stiff imitation leather.

In this case the belt buckle and the buttons are wooden, but you can buy whatever you like. Handsew the buttonholes with buttonhole silk and sew on the buttons. If you own or have access to a machine designed for sewing leather, this is a good design on which to sew all the outer stitching in buttonhole silk, making two lines of decorative stitching.

Girl's leather suit, West Greenland, late 1800s, decorated with red ribbons, red leather, and glass beads (National Museum of Denmark)

Child's dress with beadwork

Materials   Light golden sheepskin without the fleece
Long silver bugle beads
Small, round beads – blue, golden, orange, black and light blue
White buckram
Zip, 20 cm. (8 in.) long

Pattern   Page 131. Size about 9 years.

As you can see from the Greenland child's suit the tradition of setting beads on leather dates back a long way. Originally bone and amber beads were used, then coarse glass beads and now small, fine glass beads. Here I have used a flower motif taken from a 1920s garment I found in a second-hand shop, but you can of course use any design you like. You can buy lovely handmade coarse glass beads from various countries in many hobby and art shops. Remember that coarse grained leather takes coarse beads best while the kind of smooth, velvety suede used in this design goes with fine beads.

Dress   Lay the pattern on the leather. Add the seam allowance and cut out the dress. Tack it together and try it on the child. If it fits you can machine stitch the shoulder and side seams. Sew one line of gathering thread along the top of the sleeves and another along the bottom edge. Pull the gathering threads until they fit the arm opening and the child's arm. Tack in the sleeve. It is important to make sure that both sleeves are evenly 'puffed'. Stitch in the sleeves. Finish the neck opening and the bottom of the sleeves with a length of plaited leather. From the leather used for the dress cut strips 1 cm. (⅜ in.) wide, and plait as shown in the diagram.

Lay the plaited length on the leather at the neck opening and the bottom edge of the sleeves, and stitch it on by hand with invisible backstitches in the folds of the plaits. Set the zip in the dress and glue up the bottom hem to the required length.

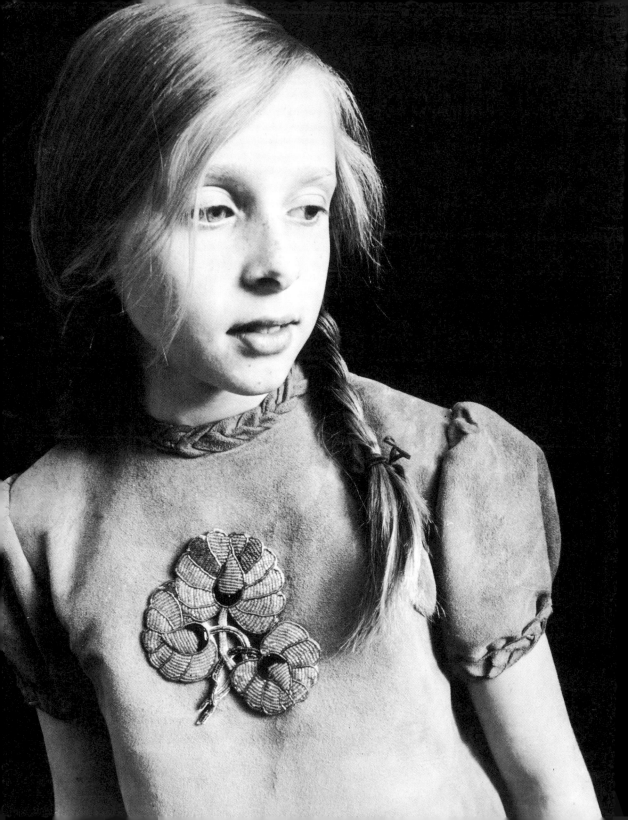

Beadwork   Draw the flower motif on paper and, using carbon paper, transfer it to the white buckram, which can be bought in a needlework shop. The beads are available in hobby shops and many department stores. We have used two sizes: small, round beads for filling in the petals, and longer ones to give a clear outline to the flower. The beads on this design are blue, golden, orange, black and light blue; the bugle beads used for the edging and the stems are silver. But the choice of colours is entirely free, provided the colours of the beads go with the colour of the leather.

Start the actual beadwork by filling in all the petals as shown in the diagram. Then start edging with the longer beads. When you have finished the beadwork, take some kind of glue which will stick glass and spread it very carefully over the back of the buckram. When it is almost dry you can pull the beads about so that they form regular rows. When the glue is completely dry cut all the surplus buckram away from the area covered by beads. Attach the beadwork to the dress with small stitches.

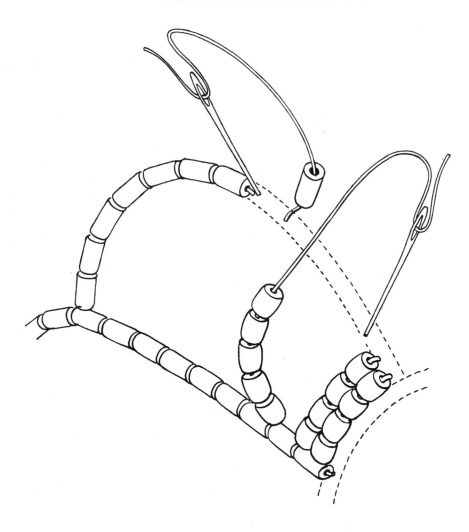

Embroidery on leather Short evening dress

Materials   1 m. black homespun fabric, 140 cm. wide (1¼ yds, 60 in. wide)
Remnants of blue leather
Embroidery wool – light and dark blue
Silk thread – light gold
2 black buckles
Zip, 35 cm. (14 in.) long

Pattern   Page 132

You can embroider on leather with many different kinds of thread and using all sorts of stitches. This design is made up in black homespun and the embroidery consists of patches of blue leather fastened on with three kinds of stitch.

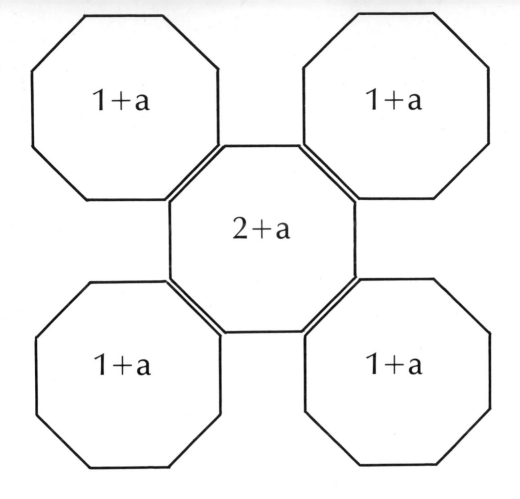

Draw up the pattern and lay it on the fabric. Add the seam allowance and cut out the dress. It is much easier to embroider the group of abstract flowers before proceeding with the basic dress.

Embroidery Cut five blue suede patches from the diagram. Stick them on to the dress with a little blob of glue. Start the embroidery with the centre flower, using both shades of blue embroidery wool: sew a dark blue French knot (a) in the centre of the flower and, with a lighter shade of blue, add lazy-daisy stitches (2) all the way round the flower as shown on the diagram. Finish by attaching the flower to the dress, using a single strand of golden silk thread. Push the needle up into the ring round the knots and down into the fabric outside the edge of the leather.

These silk threads should lie over the lazy-daisy stitches and to a certain extent cover them. The four outer flowers all contain the same stitches but differ in colour. Use light blue for two of them and darker shades of blue for the others. Sew French knots (a) in the centre of the four flowers, using blue embroidery wool for some of them and gold silk thread for one or two. Fasten on the four patches with blanket stitching (1). Make the stitches different lengths as shown in the diagram.

Dress   The centre front of the dress is decorated with a line of false saddle stitching. Tack this along both sides of the pattern pieces. Machine stitch two rows about ½ cm. (³⁄₁₆ in.) from the centre fold. The actual centre front fold stands open. Now tack the dress together and try it on. Turn the seam allowance for the top edge to the wrong side and machine stitch it down about ½ cm. (³⁄₁₆ in.) from the edge. Set facings in the arm openings. Buy two buckles the width of the straps and attach them to the dress with the pieces marked for the purpose. Attach the straps to the dress back. Set a zip in the centre back and turn up the hem with herringbone stitch.

You could of course equally well wear this dress as a pinafore dress, or over trousers.

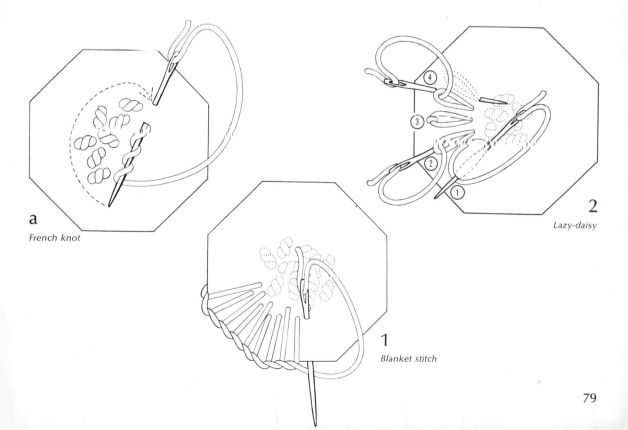

a
French knot

2
Lazy-daisy

1
Blanket stitch

Leather with fur Cloak with fox trimming

Materials
1 hunting green cowhide
Fox legs
Green leather lacing
Buckle
Zip, 120 cm. (48 in.) long

Pattern Page 133

Cloak Place the pattern on the leather, add the seam allowance and cut out the cloak. Stitch the bust and shoulder darts by machine. Neaten the hand openings by glueing down the extra seam allowance on the wrong side. 'Sew' the cloak together with leather lacing. For this design it is best to purchase green leather lacing, since ready-made lacing is usually more hard-wearing than the kind you make yourself. Now punch holes right down the side seams from shoulder to hem, so that the holes on the separate pieces lie directly over one another. They should be 1 cm. (⅜ in.) apart. When you reach the hand openings continue the row of holes down the front of the cloak. Sew the cloak together using the method of lacing shown in the diagram.

Fur Now sew the fox legs on to the cloak. It is important that they are correctly positioned, i.e. the foot of the leg should hang downwards over the cloak throughout. If the fox legs are curled and very uneven in size, wet the backs of them with water and pin them outstretched on a sheet of cardboard to dry. While the skins are wet you can form them into whatever shape you want and smooth them out. After they have dried naturally, you can use a leather knife to adjust them from the wrong side until they are uniform in length and width. But cut carefully from the wrong side so as not to damage the fur on the right side. Start actually attaching the fur from the centre back, turning two fox legs towards each other. Fasten the skins with pins.

You should stitch the fur with a darning needle or a special leather needle and strong thread. A steel thimble will be needed. Sew the skins on by hand with ordinary running stitches. This work is hard on the hands so it is sensible to stop for a while every now and again. Glue up the bottom edge of the cloak. You can fasten the front with hooks or a zip. You will

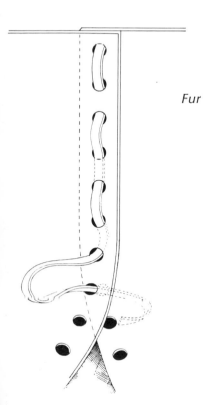

probably have to order the zip specially to get the right colour and length, but the advantage of using a zip rather than hooks is that it will keep the cloak properly fastened. On this model we have added a buckle. This can obviously be omitted, but if you do want something like it you should attach it by cutting a strip of leather the same width as the buckle, slitting the cloak, putting the leather strip round the buckle and glueing the strip to the wrong side of the cloak.

If you want to line the cloak you can buy quilted nylon lining, cut it from the pattern and stitch it into the cloak. If you don't want any lining, you can neaten the back of the cloak by sticking on a facing of thin leather to cover the stitching which fastens the fox leg trim.

Beret   Cut six panels from the pattern. Then punch holes about 1 cm. (⅜ in.) apart and ¾ cm. (¼ in.) in from the edge of the leather. Use green leather lacing to join the hat together, following the same method as for the cloak. Then cut a strip of leather about 3 cm. (1⅛ in.) wide and long enough to fit round the head. Wrap the strip round your head to fit snugly and mark off the correct length. When you have adjusted the hatband, glue it into the beret. You can make small gathers in the main body of the hat so that it fits neatly into the hatband.

Boy's suit with branded autographs

Materials	1 beige cowhide Branding tools Zip, 20 cm. (8 in.) long
Pattern	Page 134. Size about 12 years.

Trousers When you have drawn up the pattern, lay it on the leather, add the seam allowance and cut out. Tack the trousers together and fit. It is important that the top part of the trousers sits tightly, in contrast to the flare. When you have adjusted the trousers, sew them together. If you own a machine which sews leather easily, you can join the top part of the trousers to the flare with a row of top stitching. If, on the other hand, your machine has difficulty sewing leather, a line of irregular stitches won't look very attractive, so it is wiser to handsew with running stitches (preferably in coloured buttonhole silk to match the leather). Then stitch all seams by machine. Set a zip in the centre front, either by hand or machine. If you want to use a belt, finish the trousers by adding loops. Clip the seam allowance on the wrong side so that it doesn't pull creases in the trousers.

Waistcoat Stitch the yokes to the front and back pieces. Then try the waistcoat on. If it fits, stitch all seams. Cut all the facings out. These can be machine stitched on from the right side, if your machine can manage it, otherwise you will have to work by hand. Now cut the fringe with scissors or a leather knife. Use a steel rule to get them completely straight and uniform.

Branding Most hobby shops stock very reasonably-priced branding tools. Plug the tool into the mains and use it like an ordinary fountain pen. Don't press down but just guide the pen over the leather. Obviously the names used in this design are only a suggestion, and you can use your own imagination.

Lambskin waistcoat with appliqué motif

Appliqué I

Materials
1 piece of golden lambskin with the fleece on
Lime-green suede
Leather lacing
Eyelets

Pattern
Page 135

Lay the pattern on the lambskin. There is no need to add a seam allowance as the waistcoat is laced together. Cut the lambskin from the leather side with a knife, taking care not to damage the fleece on the wrong side. If you do the cutting properly the fleece will hang naturally over the leather side making a good edge.

Appliqué
Draw up the leaf motif from the pattern and use carbon paper to transfer it to the lime-green suede. Each square should measure 5 cm. (2 in.). Remember to reverse the right and left sides. Using leather glue, carefully stick the motifs to the two front pieces of the waistcoat.

    Now punch holes in the shoulder and side seams about 1½ cm. (⅝ in.) from each other and the same distance in from the edge of the leather. Place brass eyelets in these holes. You can press them down with the punch shown on page 15. If you don't own a tool of this kind any leather dealer should be able to do this for you. When you have done all the eyelets, cut a strip of leather lacing about ½ cm. (³⁄₁₆ in.) wide from the green suede, and lace the waistcoat together as you would lace a shoe. Finish off with a knot or bow. On the model shown here the back of the waistcoat has the fleece as the right side. If you get tired of this, you can just change the back piece round.

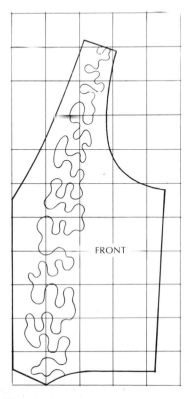

FRONT

Appliqué II Long skirt and waistcoat with appliqué flower motif

Materials Blue-green sheepskin
           Suede pieces – red, green and yellow
           Rivets
           Press studs

Pattern   Page 136

As you can see from the photograph of this delightful hat from Greenland, appliqué work is an extremely old technique.

Conical hat with leather cut-out figures sewn on. Angmagsalik, late 1800s (National Museum of Denmark)

Draw up the pattern and lay it on the leather. Add the seam allowance and cut out.

Waistcoat   Tack the darts and seams and try the waistcoat on. If it fits, machine stitch it together. The edge of the waistcoat is decorated with a sort of scallop which you can make with a punch. Cut some 'half holes' along the edge of the waistcoat with the thickest pipe on the punch so that you get a scalloped edge. Although this edging is undoubtedly attractive it is only suitable for firm leather of good quality. When using cheaper kinds of leather use ordinary facings.

Skirt   Tack the skirt panels together and try it on. Then machine stitch the seams. Cut the broad waistband double. On the wrong side of the waistband the smooth side of the leather faces up. Stitch the waistband, turn and sew it on to the skirt. Lay it on the skirt, right sides together, stitch, turn to the wrong side and fasten down. You can glue the edge of the leather if it is too thick to fold. Fasten the skirt in the centre front seam with press studs which you can either put in yourself, following the instructions on page 111, or get the leather dealer to insert for you. Finish the hem with a scalloped edge as for the jerkin.

Appliqué   Make the appliqué flower motif in the following way: using the diagram as a pattern draw the flowers on to leather of three different colours. The flower in this design is worked in yellow, green and red (from the centre) so that with the blue background it keeps to the classic colour scheme of folk costume. There are ten flowers altogether. Lay the three pieces on top of each other and turn until the petals fit into one another. Glue them on to the skirt and the jerkin. Punch a hole in the centre of the flower to go right through the backing of the jerkin or skirt. Set a rivet in this hole and bang it flat with a hammer on a hard surface.

Patchwork collage I Long skirt

Materials An old brown suede coat
Light brown suede split
Red-brown suede split
Buttons

Pattern Page 137

Skirt The materials for this design consist of an old suede coat with all the worn patches cut out, and two comparatively cheap pieces of suede split in colours to tone with the coat.

Make a template 15 × 15 cm. (6 × 6 in.) out of cardboard and draw the required number of squares from it. Cut them out with scissors or a knife. Thread the sewing machine with a different coloured but toning thread, and sew in a zigzag stitch with the needle in the position of maximum swing. Lay the squares edge to edge and sew backwards and forwards a few times to strengthen the seam. Sew up the back and the two fronts of the skirt separately. Then stitch the darts, which are placed at the join between two panels to make them look smooth from the right side. Sew the side seams of the skirt with straight stitching. Cut out the front facings and the waistband according to the pattern. Lay the front facings right sides down on the right sides of the skirt fronts. Stitch them on and turn to the wrong side. Fasten them down by sewing two lines of stitching the width of the pressure foot from the edge. Sew on the waistband in the same way. Finish the skirt off with buttons, which you can make yourself from the instructions on page 111, and buttonholes handsewn with buttonhole thread. Turn up the skirt by glueing up the hem to the required length.

Patchwork collage II # Jacket of leather remnants

Materials   Suede remnants
            Lining
            Nylon fur trimming
            Jacket hooks

Pattern   Page 138

This jacket is a good example of the use of remnants. Since it is also trimmed with nylon fur it is particularly reasonable in price.

Jacket   Draw up the pattern. Now start sewing the suede remnants together. Cut the pieces so that they fit together. The easiest way to do this is by laying the pieces of leather over each other and cutting through both pieces along what will be the stitching line. When you take them apart the pieces will fit. Pay attention to the blend of colours and try to achieve balance among the pieces as you choose them. Then zigzag the pieces together until you have lengths large enough to cover the individual pattern pieces plus a seam allowance.

We have used brown thread for this jacket since the fur is brown. Stitch backwards and forwards a couple of times to make the joins stronger. When you have finished making up the lengths, place the pattern pieces on top. Add the seam allowance and cut the jacket out. Then tack together and try it on. Now machine stitch along all the seams. Cut out and stitch the lining, making sure that it comes right out to the edges so that the jacket doesn't pull tight. We have used a woolly lining from an old coat. Set it in the jacket and handsew the edges together down the front, round the neck opening and along the hem. Sew on the fur trim at the same time. You can buy this by the yard in department stores or needlework shops. Finish the sleeves of the jacket in the same way. Sew the hooks in the jacket front.

95

Girl's skirt with suede patches

Materials   Green flannel, 70 × 100 cm. (20 × 54 in.)
Suede remnants
Rivets
Zip, 20 cm. (8 in.) long

Pattern   Page 139. Size about 12 years.

When you have been working with leather for a while the time
will come when you've collected a bag full of remnants. You
can also buy bags of pieces comparatively cheaply from many
leather dealers. This design is one experiment in using
remnants in a decorative way.

Skirt   The basic material in this design is green flannel, but you can
use many other kinds of fabric as long as they take the patches
without stretching. Draw the pattern on to paper and lay it on
the material. Add a seam allowance and cut out the skirt. Tack
it together and try it on. When you have made any adjustments
necessary, stitch all darts and seams. The waistband of the skirt
is fairly deep. Cut this out double and lay it on the skirt right
sides together. Stitch the waistband in place, turn it to the
wrong side of the skirt and hem it down by hand. Set a zip in
the centre back seam to fasten the skirt.

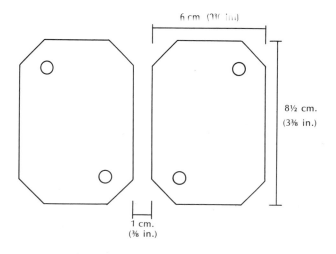

6 cm. (2¼ in.)

8½ cm.
(3⅜ in.)

1 cm.
(⅜ in.)

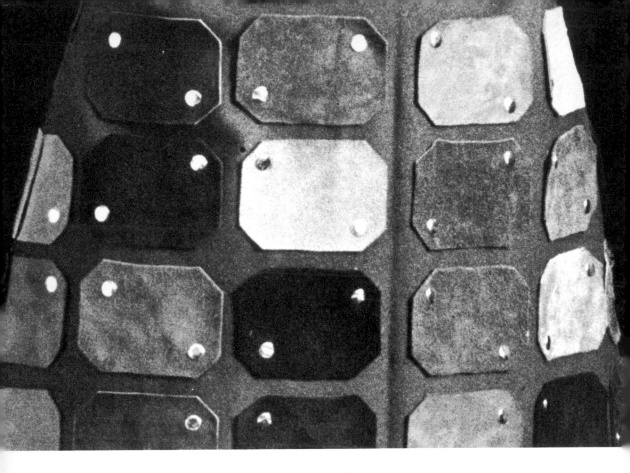

Suede patches Make a cardboard template from the diagram. Now lay this template on the wrong side of whatever suede remnants you have. Draw round the template with a biro. Then cut out all the patches, using either scissors or a knife. Place the patches on the skirt so that the colours harmonize, and stick them on with leather glue. A problem will arise when you come to the side seams of the skirt since they are not cut straight. Here you should lay on the patches, mark the position of the seams on the suede and cut the patches to fit the seams. To heighten the effect, and to ensure the patches stay on, we have used rivets. For the positioning of these see the photograph. To insert them, start by making a hole with a punch, stick the rivet firmly into place and hit it with a hammer. Use something hard to rest the work on. A saucepan is fine for this as you can draw the skirt down round it.

Gloves

Materials Red nappa glove leather
Zip, 10 cm. (4 in.) long
Zip ring

Pattern Page 140

Gloves Draw the pattern for the gloves on to cardboard. Lay your hand over the pattern so that you can compare your size with it. Make the pattern larger or smaller as necessary. Cut out the gloves.

   Place the pattern on the leather so that the leather stretches across the hand as shown in the diagram. Remember to cut out one right and one left hand! Handsew the gloves together using a running stitch which looks the same size on both the front and the back of the gloves. Use buttonhole silk to match the colour of the leather. Start sewing from the wrist, and stitch from the wrist to the tip of the little finger. Now take two of the

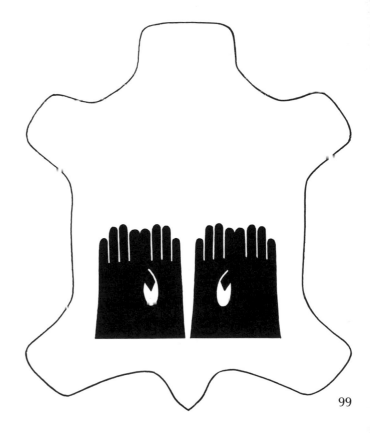

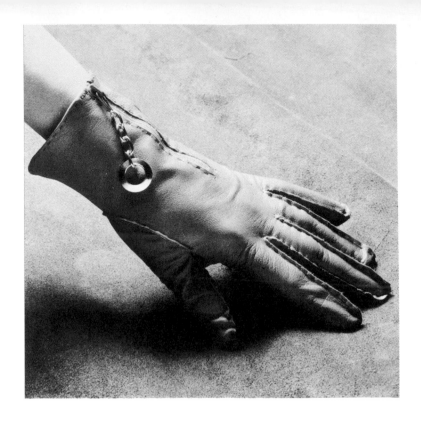

small pieces of leather used to cover the gaps between the fingers. Join them at the straight edge, right sides together. Fasten the finger gussets into the glove with the seam at the bottom of the space between the little and fourth fingers. One gusset is used for the little finger, the other for the fourth finger. First stitch up the side of the little finger. Cut the gusset to the required length and attach it to the tip of the little finger. Continue with the next finger. You will need three double gussets for each glove. When you have finished the four fingers the thumb will still be left to do. Cut this out. Start sewing the thumb together at the tip and continue right the way round. Finish the glove by cutting a slit for the zip. Turn the hem allowance on the glove to the wrong side at the wrist, and make a line of small running stitches from the right side in order to hold it. Start sewing on the little finger side, stitch up to and round the zip and carry on round the back of the hand. You can make the glove more attractive by attaching a small chain with a ring to the zip. You can buy this kind of thing in the haberdashery department of a large store.

Slipper boots

Materials   Red suede split
Sealskin
Blue nappa glove leather
2 felt soles in whatever size shoe you take
Zip, 30 cm. (12 in.) long

Pattern   Page 141

When you look at photographs of boots or slippers you probably imagine they are difficult to make, but that isn't in fact the case. As long as you follow the instructions you shouldn't encounter any problems.

Slipper boots   Draw up the pattern from the diagram, to fit your feet. Lay the pattern on the leather (we have deliberately chosen a fairly

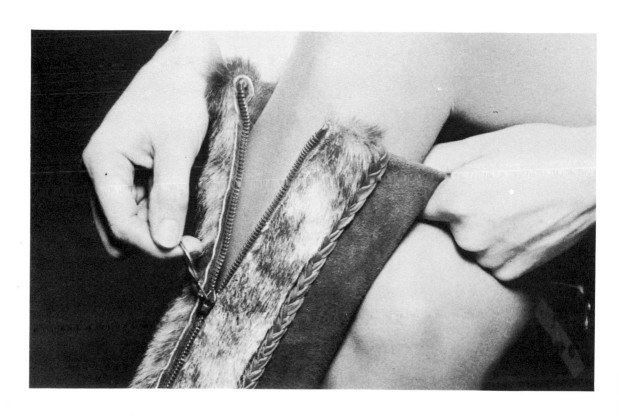

strong suede), add the seam allowance and cut out the uppers. Stitch the back seam on a sewing machine. Now stitch up the front seam, leaving space for the zip. In the design shown here we have trimmed the front of the boots with sealskin. You can obviously omit this or replace it with imitation fur, as you wish. Cut the strips of sealskin 3 cm. (1⅛ in.) wide and glue them on to the boots. Cover the edge of the sealskin with a plait of blue nappa glove leather (see the diagram on page 71 for how the plaiting is done). Buy some felt soles with a little heel, of the kind specially designed for slippers. Draw the uppers down over the soles and sew them on with strong thread. Insert the needle up and down through the sole, stitching firmly so that the boots will stand up to wear. Cover the stitching with a plait of leather, stuck on with glue. Glue down the top edge of the uppers to the required length. Finish the boots by either glue-ing or sewing in the zip down the centre front. The best way to go about this is to stick the zip in first with a little glue, and then handsew a line of backstitching down the sides to strengthen the glue. You can buy from your leather dealer various decora-tive attachments to hang from the zip.

Duffle coat with braided fastening

Materials   Brown lambskin with the fleece on
1 piece green lambskin with the fleece on
Brown suede remnants
Leather lacing

Pattern   Page 142

Braided fastening

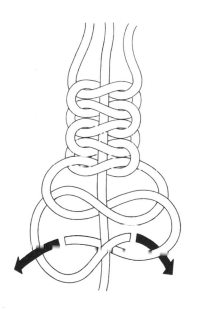

Draw up the pattern and lay the yoke and cuffs on the green lambskin and all the rest on the brown lambskin. Add the seam allowance and start cutting out the coat. Don't cut the lambskin with scissors, but with a leather knife so as not to damage the fleece, for in this design the wool shows round the leather like a white stripe to provide a decorative edge. This means that when you put the garment together, you shouldn't lay the individual pieces right sides together before sewing them, as you would normally, but lay the seam allowance of one piece over the seam allowance of the other and then tack the garment together. Try the jacket on. If it fits, machine stitch it together on the right side with two rows of stitching about ½ cm. (¼ in.) apart. You might think it would be a hard job to pass thick leather of this kind through the machine, but it should slip through quite easily. Set the sleeves in, again stitching from the outside. Attach the collar to the neck of the jacket and the front lapel, taking the fleece as the right side. You should do this by hand, making the stitches as invisible as you can. Machine stitching would spoil the appearance of the jacket. The same applies to the green cuffs, so handsew these to the sleeves. Make the buttons for this design from the instructions on page 110.

Start by plaiting the leather lacing into a strip 8 cm. (3¼ in.) long. Tie this to something firm, a door handle for example, then take the middle lace and fix it to a belt tied round your waist. Following the diagram, knot a piece 13 cm. (5 in.) long. Then untie the middle lace and plait for 8 cm. (3¼ in.). Plaiting is illustrated on page 71. When you have finished the last piece of plaiting, glue the ends of the two plaited strips firmly to the back of the knotted length. This will make two loops which serve as buttonholes.

Long dress with braided belt

Materials   Good quality firm chamois leather
Leather lacing
Buckles

Pattern   Page 143

The pattern for this model is quite simple. The design is taken from a woman's dress of the Iron Age. The belt is a whipcord, which was also worn during the Iron Age.

Dress   Take the separate skins and zigzag them together on a sewing machine, using thread the same colour as the leather. Sew them together into the shape of a tube. The length of the tube will be the length of the dress plus a piece about 25 cm. (10 in.) long which will make a kind of casual wrapover scarf. It is important that the natural irregularities in the leather should be used to form the top and bottom edges of the tube. If they seem too uneven you will have to help nature a bit and straighten the edges slightly. Fasten the dress on the shoulders with two buckles.

Whipcord   Buy leather lacing at a leather merchant. Tie four laces to something firm, a door handle for example, and then proceed as shown in the diagrams.

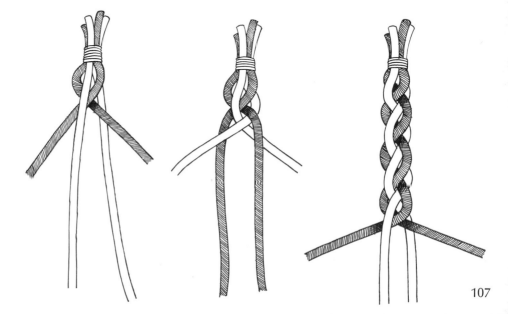

Button Making

Often it is some small detail which makes a picture complete. With home-made garments this detail can be matching buttons, and the photograph shows various examples of these. The following list of instructions for making them starts with the button in the top left corner.

1.   If you want to do it the easy way, you can just take along to a leather dealer a piece of leather which matches the garment. Most dealers will agree to cover buttons for you. Even so the buttons will not look like something you have just bought from a shop, because the leather will be exactly the same as is used for the garment.

2.   For this button use a curtain ring of the diameter you want the button to be. Cut out a piece of leather slightly larger than the size of the ring. Make a line of running stitches round the

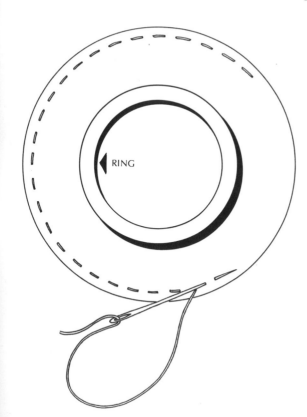

RING

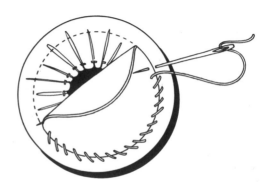

edge of the leather with tacking thread. Pull the thread to gather the leather round the ring (see the diagram). Now cover the surplus leather at the back of the button with a piece of leather cut to the size of the ring. This piece will form the back of the button. Sew it on with small hemming stitches. Make a decorative ring of back stitches on the right side of the button just inside the curtain ring, using thread to match the garment.

3. This is simply a variation of button number 2. Make the basic button in the same way but embroider a little flower on the leather first. The flower is composed of lazy-daisy stitch and French knots. Both these stitches are illustrated in the diagram on page 79.

4. This is also a variation of button number 2. The basic method is the same. The decoration is made from a curtain ring small enough to fit just inside the outer ring of the button. Cover the inner ring with a circle of close stitching, using thread to match the garment.

5. The design in the top right-hand corner, which is shown in two stages, is not very difficult to make. Admittedly it looks a

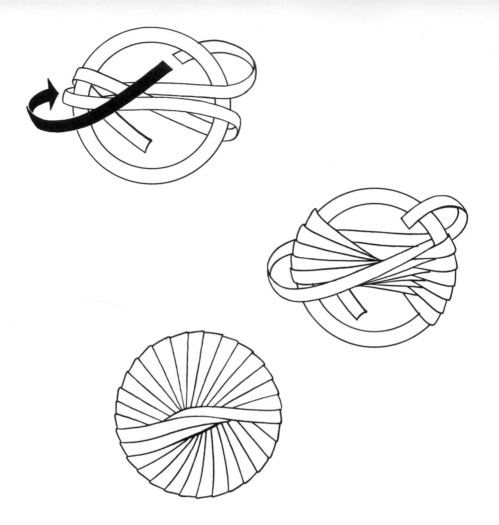

little complicated but it is very attractive when finished. Cut a long strip of leather ¼ cm. (⅛ in.) wide from a soft and preferably thin kind of leather. Chamois or good quality glove leather are ideal. Then start making the button as shown in the diagrams. Fasten the end on the wrong side.

6. The design on the far left of the second row is the classic toggle as used on duffle coats. Following the diagram, cut out a piece of leather and roll it up, possibly with the addition of a little glue. Attach the button with a strip of leather passed round the button and fastened through a slit in the garment. Glue down the strip on the back. You can make this kind of button in any size by just making the pattern in the diagram larger or smaller.

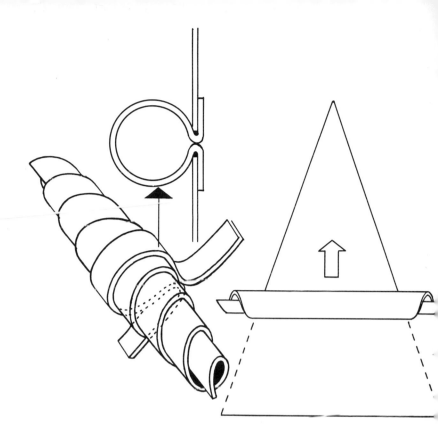

7. This is a home-made covered button. You can buy the basic button trims in the haberdashery department of any store, and at many leather dealers. Just cut out a circular piece of leather a little larger than the actual button trim, gather the extra leather into the back of the button and push the back part of the trim down on to the outer half of the button. We have used this kind of button for the chamois bikini.

8. Press studs – you can either ask the leather dealer to hammer these in or buy them from him and put them in yourself. They are sold complete with the two small tools for inserting the stud, which are shown in the photograph. Press studs are especially suitable for use in teaching because they are so much easier than buttons and buttonholes. In this book we have used press studs for several designs.

How to use the patterns

This section contains a brief explanation of how to take measurements, how to draw up the patterns and how to adjust the basic pattern. Unfortunately this is bound to be no more than a summary. For detailed information on the subject you should consult books on dressmaking, which you should be able to find quite easily in your local public library.

Taking measurements

The one essential for using any pattern is meticulous measurement. You can't do this properly on your own but must have someone else to help you. To make it easier you can tie a narrow tape round your waist, making sure that it is exactly at the waist. And to find the correct place for the back measurement you can put on a necklace and measure from that.

You can then take the most important measurements which are the following:

Bust: Measure round the body at the fullest part of the bust, but without pulling the tape tight. If you wish, you can curve the tape measure slightly upwards at the back to allow room for movement.

Waist: Measure round the body exactly at the waistline.

Hips: Measure round the broadest part of the hips.

Back length: Measure from the nape of the neck to the waistline.

Back width: Measure across the breadth of the back from where the arm joins the body.

Bust height: Measure from the shoulder at the neck side to the fullest point of the bust.

Arm length: Bend your arm slightly and measure under the arm from armpit to wrist.

Length of skirt: From the waist to the required length

Inside leg length: Used for trousers. Measure from the crotch to the bottom edge of the trousers.

When you have taken these measurements write them in the measurement chart. Then compare them with the standard measurements and list any differences with a plus or a minus sign.

Measurement chart

	Book measurements	Personal measurements
Bust	92 cm. (36 in.)	
Waist	66 cm. (26 in.)	
Hips	96 cm. (38 in.)	
Back length	42 cm. (16½ in.)	
Back width	38 cm. (15 in.)	
Bust height	22½ cm. (9 in.)	
Arm length	varies	
Skirt length	varies	
Inside leg length	varies	

As you can see from the measurement chart the great majority of the garments in this book are designed to fit what is considered an average size, which means women's size 36 (size 14 in the UK, size 12 in the USA). Garments for children and men have the size on the instructions.

Drawing up the pattern

In the last section of the book you will find a pattern for every garment illustrated. You should draw up the pattern on squared paper, each square being 5 × 5 cm. (2 × 2 in.). Remember that each pattern piece must be cut out twice, the second time with the pattern turned over. When you want to transfer the pattern from the book, go to a stationer and buy squared paper which is divided into millimetres, centimetres, and finally with heavier lines for every 5 cm., which is what you need most of. If the paper isn't large enough you can stick several sheets together with Sellotape. Now draw the pattern from the book on to the squared paper. You may think this is difficult but it is actually amazingly simple, though obviously you will have to work very accurately. Before cutting out the individual pattern pieces you should compare the measurements of the design with your own measurement chart.

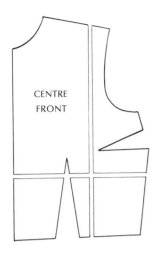

CENTRE FRONT

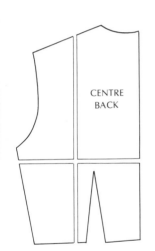

CENTRE BACK

Adjusting the pattern

When making a decision about which size to choose, you start from your bust measurement for blouses and dresses, and from the hip measurement for trousers and skirts. If this measurement falls between two standard sizes you will have to adjust the pattern. There are two ways of doing this, depending on whether you are making the pattern larger or smaller. If the difference in size is only a small one, there is no reason why you shouldn't either add to or subtract from the pattern, at the side seams for instance.

It is all too easy, however, to throw out the whole balance of the design, so in many cases you may find it preferable to cut the pattern and spread the pieces, if it is to be made larger, or fold it, if it is to be reduced. The diagrams show one way in which you can cut out and spread the pattern. As you can see, there is a limit on how far you can spread the pattern without all the dimensions becoming distorted. If the discrepancy between your size and the one used in the book is too great, the best solution is to buy a ready-made pattern to fit your own personal measurements. We have not illustrated how to reduce a pattern by folding it but the procedure is the same as for making it larger. All you need to remember is to fold along the cutting lines until the pattern is the required size.

When you have drawn up the pattern and adjusted it, if necessary, we would always recommend you to stick together half the garment (half the pattern drawn up in tissue paper) with Sellotape and try it on.

Seam allowance: Reckon extra seam allowance as follows: 1 cm. (⅜ in.) at neck and armholes, collar and cuffs; 2 cm. (⅞ in.) at the shoulders; 2–3 cm. (⅞–1⅛ in.) at the side seams. Allow 5 cm. (2 in.) for turning up the hem.

Placing the pattern on the leather: Leather has no nap to be taken into account, but take care with suede. Remember when it comes to positioning the pattern pieces that you can save leather by experimenting with the position of individual pieces. Remember, also, to look at the right side of the leather in case any faults in the hide show up too distinctly on the finished garment.

The patterns

Waistcoat suit – short pants with long waistcoat

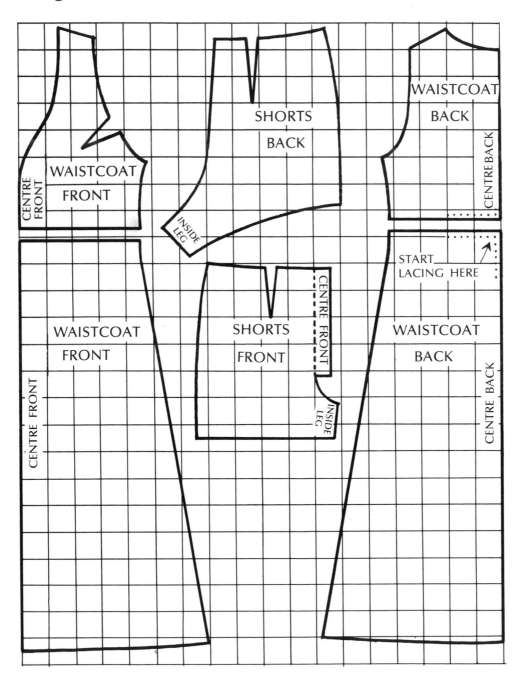

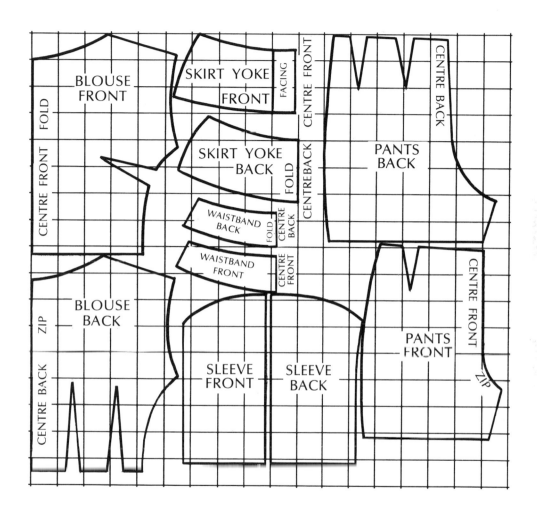

Red leather jerkin with painted peasant motif

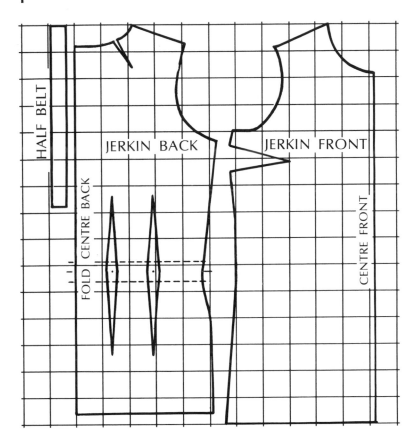

HALF BELT

JERKIN BACK

JERKIN FRONT

FOLD CENTRE BACK

CENTRE FRONT

Man's waistcoat with printed motif

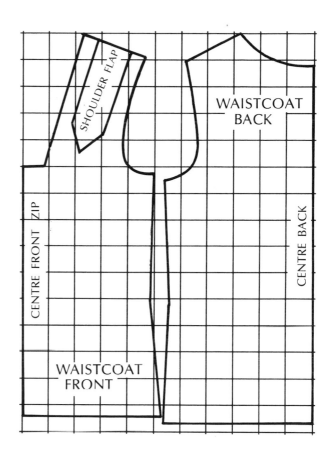

Boy's waistcoat with printed motifs

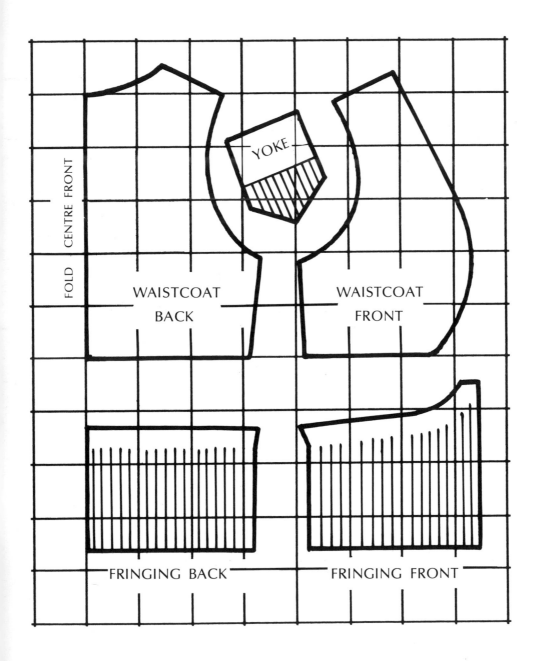

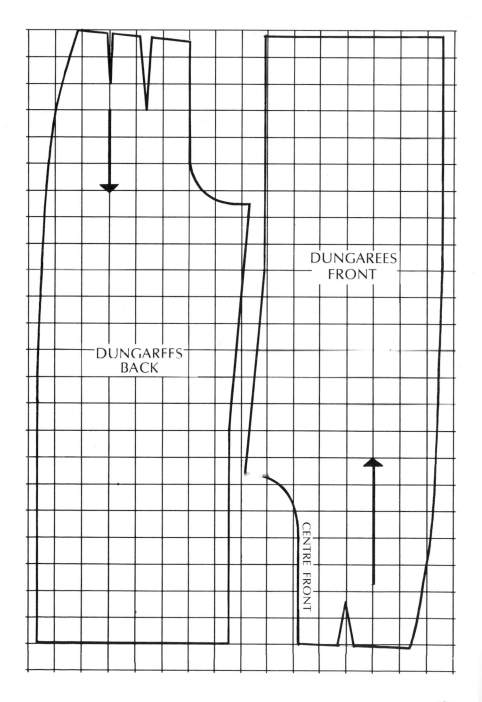

DUNGAREES
FRONT

DUNGAREES
BACK

CENTRE FRONT

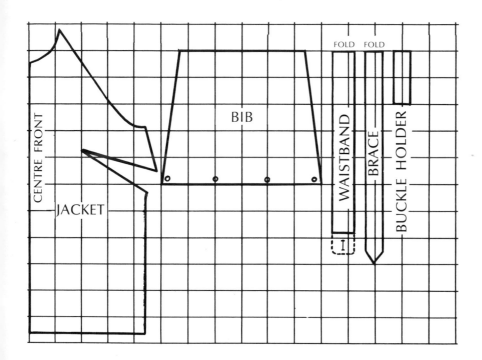

CENTRE FRONT

BIB

JACKET

FOLD   FOLD

WAISTBAND

BRACE

BUCKLE HOLDER

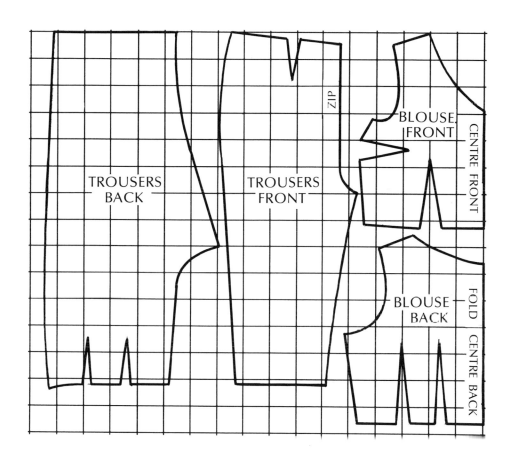

Midi dress with Greenland leather embroidery

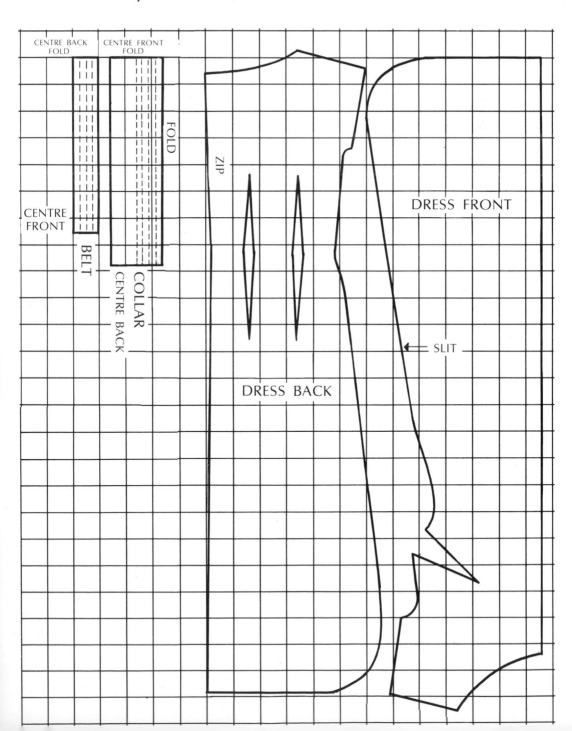

CENTRE BACK FOLD

CENTRE FRONT FOLD

FOLD

ZIP

CENTRE FRONT

BELT

COLLAR

CENTRE BACK

DRESS FRONT

SLIT

DRESS BACK

White anorak with Greenland leather embroidery

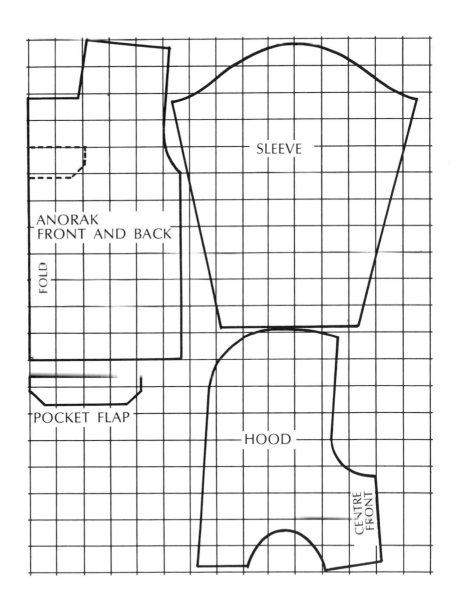

Red shirt and skirt with Greenland leather embroidery

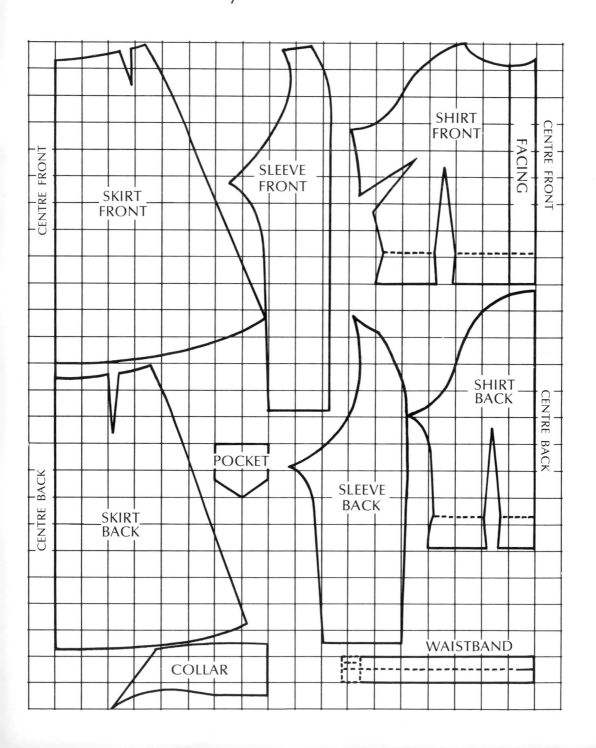

CENTRE FRONT

SKIRT FRONT

SLEEVE FRONT

SHIRT FRONT

FACING

CENTRE FRONT

POCKET

SKIRT BACK

CENTRE BACK

SLEEVE BACK

SHIRT BACK

CENTRE BACK

COLLAR

WAISTBAND

Pigskin skirt with quilted cable motif

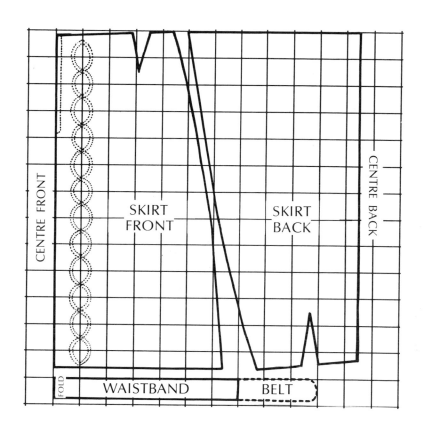

Quilted chamois bikini

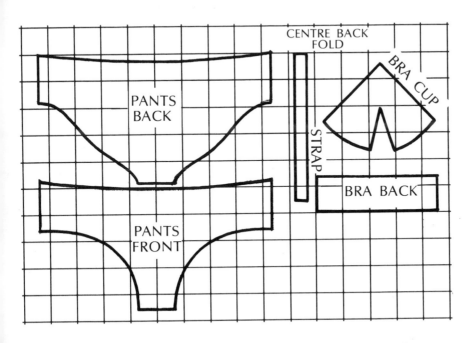

CENTRE BACK
FOLD

PANTS
BACK

STRAP

BRA CUP

BRA BACK

PANTS
FRONT

Slipover with Cretan pattern

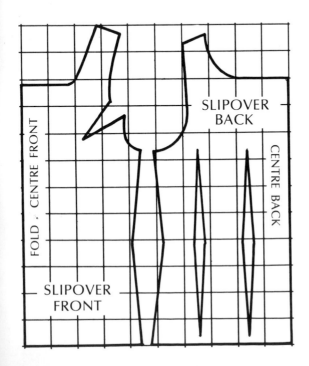

SLIPOVER
BACK

FOLD · CENTRE FRONT

CENTRE BACK

SLIPOVER
FRONT

Safari suit with diamond motif in leather mosaic

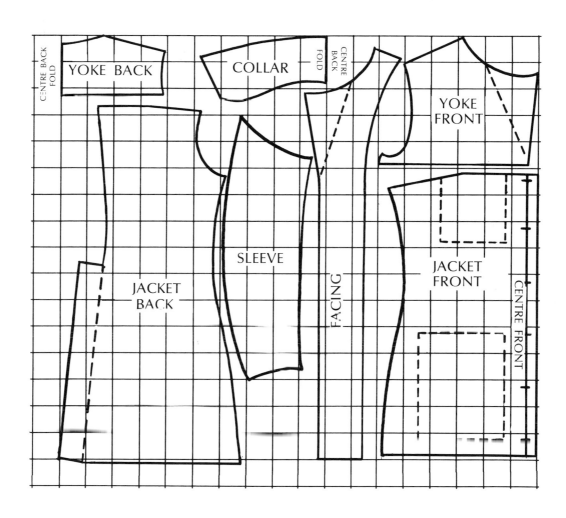

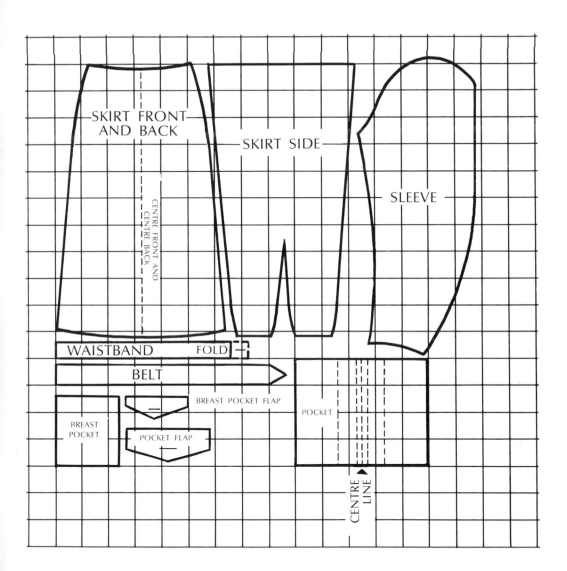

SKIRT FRONT AND BACK

CENTRE FRONT AND CENTRE BACK

SKIRT SIDE

SLEEVE

WAISTBAND   FOLD

BELT

BREAST POCKET FLAP

BREAST POCKET

POCKET FLAP

POCKET

CENTRE LINE

Child's dress with beadwork

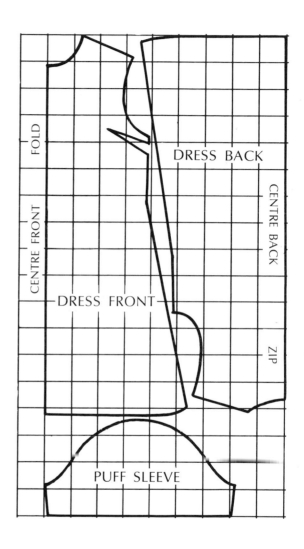

Short evening dress

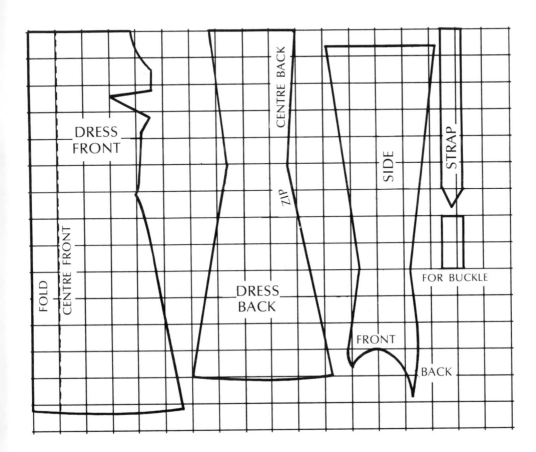

Cloak with fox trimming

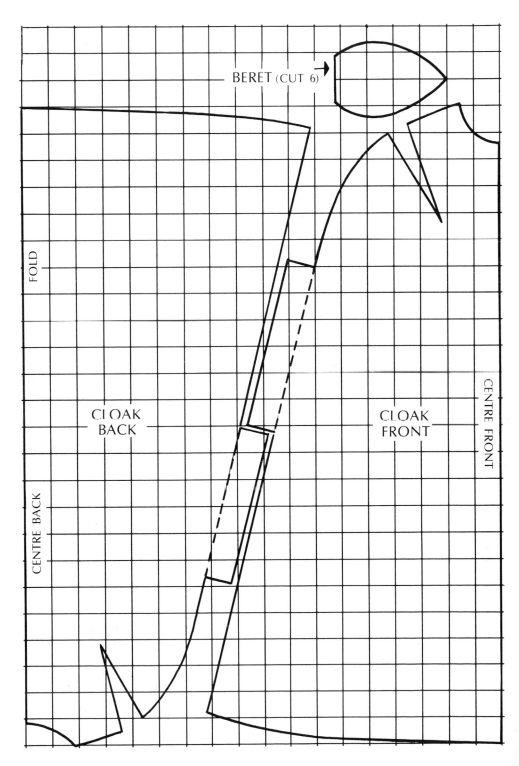

BERET (CUT 6)

FOLD

CENTRE BACK

CLOAK
BACK

CLOAK
FRONT

CENTRE FRONT

Boy's suit with branded autographs

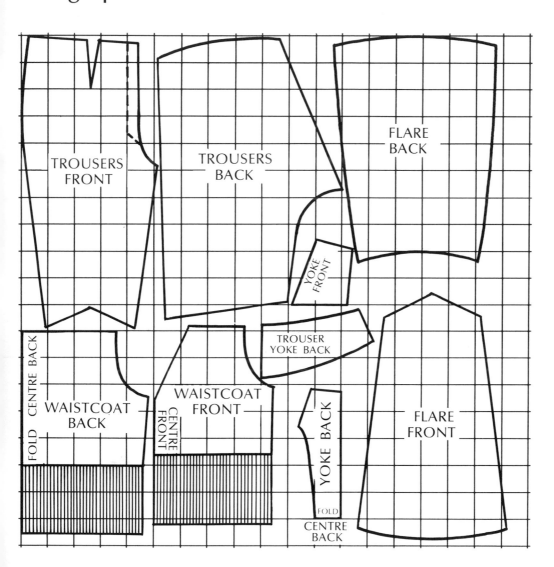

Lambskin waistcoat with appliqué motif

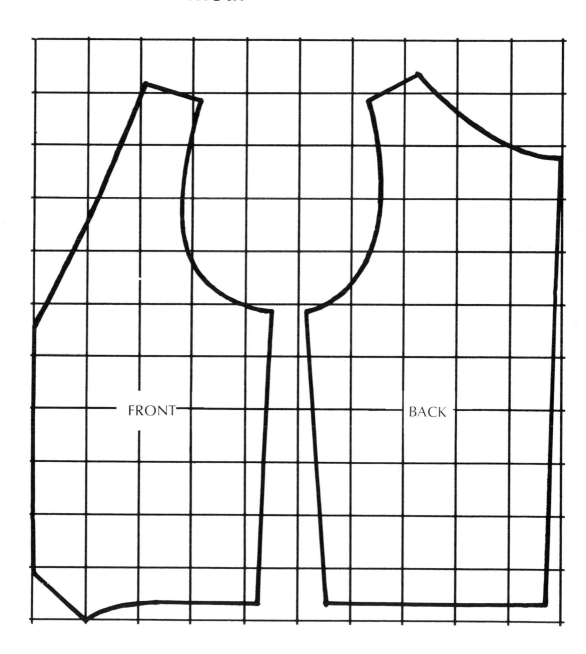

FRONT

BACK

Long skirt and waistcoat with appliqué flower motif

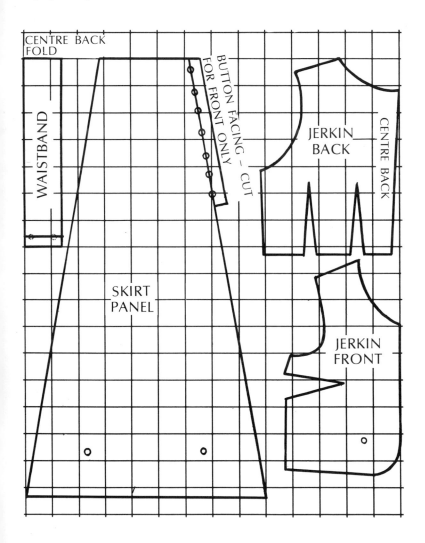

CENTRE BACK FOLD

WAISTBAND

BUTTON FACING – CUT FOR FRONT ONLY

SKIRT PANEL

JERKIN BACK

CENTRE BACK

JERKIN FRONT

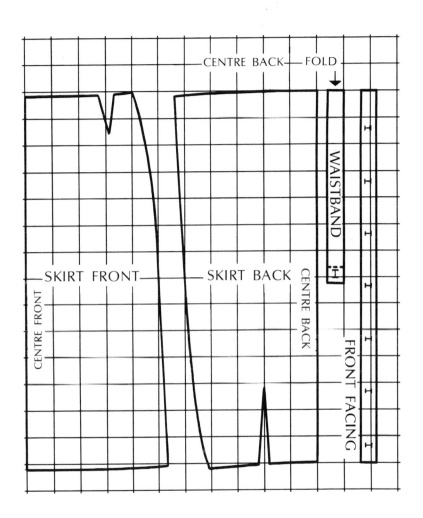

Jacket of leather remnants

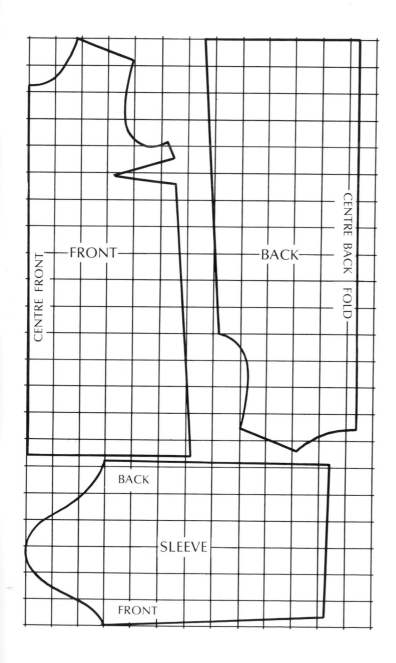

Girl's skirt with suede patches

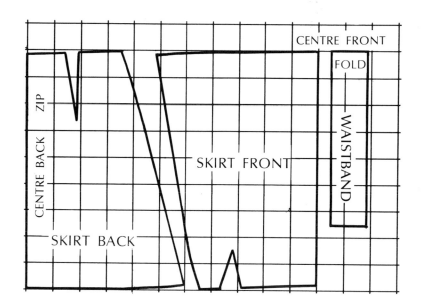

CENTRE FRONT

FOLD

WAISTBAND

ZIP

CENTRE BACK

SKIRT FRONT

SKIRT BACK

Gloves

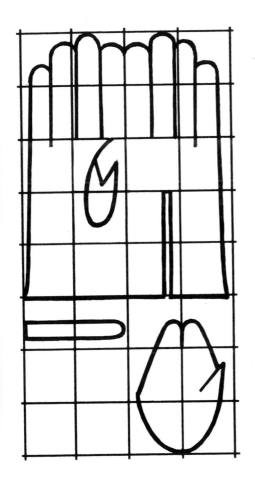

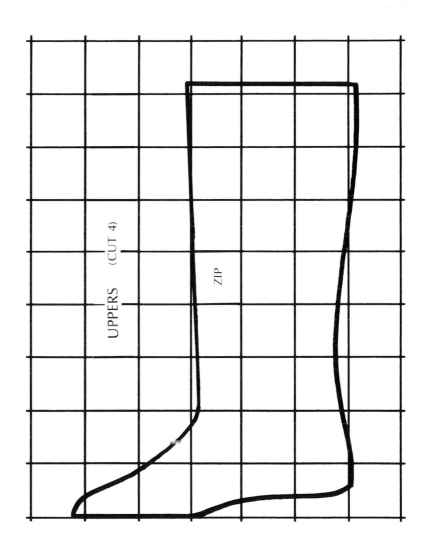

UPPERS (CUT 4)

ZIP

Duffle coat with braided fastening

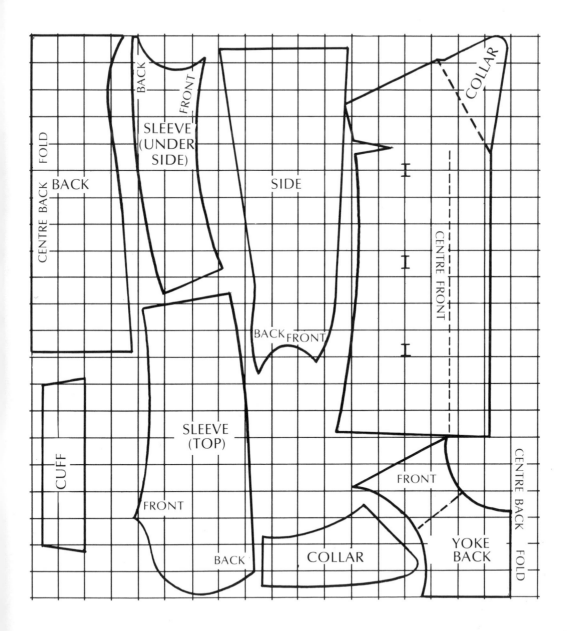

Long dress with braided belt

FLAPOVER
PIECE

FRONT
AND BACK

CENTRE FRONT

CENTRE BACK

FOLD

Suppliers

UK

Hides and remnants
Alma (London) Ltd., 18 Clerkenwell Rd., London EC1
Connolly Bros. Ltd., 39 Chalton St., London NW1
C. G. Honeywill Ltd., 32 Carnaby St., London W1
Light Leather Co. Ltd., 18 Newman St., London W1

Mail Order
The Tannery Shop, Gomshall, Guildford, Surrey

Tools
Taylor & Co. Ltd., 54 Old St., London EC1

USA

Hides
AC Products, 422 Hudson St., New York, N.Y. 10014
Charles Horowitz & Sons Inc., 25 Great Jones St., New York,
    N.Y. 10012
    (both these suppliers sell whole hides only)

Hides and remnants
Bill Levine Leather Corp., 17 Cleveland Place, New York,
    N.Y. 10012
    (specialises in scrap leather)
MacLeather Company, 424 Broome St., New York, N.Y. 10013
Tandy Leather Company Inc., Box 791, Fort Worth, Texas 76101
    (also has more than 140 retail stores throughout the USA)

Tools
Charles Horowitz & Sons Ltd.
Bill Levine Leather Corp.
Tandy Leather Company Inc.

All the above USA suppliers are both mail order and retail

Supplers